UPSIDE DOWN FOOTBALL

UPSIDE DOWN FOOTBALL

An Inside Look at Long Snapping in the NFL

Ted Kluck

ROWMAN & LITTLEFIELD
Lanham • Boulder • New York • London

Published by Rowman & Littlefield
A wholly owned subsidiary of The Rowman & Littlefield Publishing Group,
Inc.
4501 Forbes Boulevard, Suite 200, Lanham, Maryland 20706
www.rowman.com

Unit A, Whitacre Mews, 26-34 Stannary Street, London SE11 4AB

British Library Cataloguing in Publication Information Available

Library of Congress Cataloging-in-Publication Data

Names: Kluck, Ted, author.
Title: Upside down football : an inside look at long snapping in the NFL / Ted Kluck.
Description: Lanham : Rowman & Littlefield, [2017] | Includes bibliographical references.
Identifiers: LCCN 2016022202 (print) | LCCN 2016040269 (ebook) | ISBN 9781442257115
    (cloth : alk. paper) | ISBN 9781442257122 (electronic)
Subjects: LCSH: Special teams (Football)
Classification: LCC GV951.85 .K58 2017 (print) | LCC GV951.85 (ebook) | DDC 796.332/2—dc23
    LC record available at https://lccn.loc.gov/2016022202

∞ ™ The paper used in this publication meets the minimum requirements of
American National Standard for Information Sciences Permanence of Paper
for Printed Library Materials, ANSI/NISO Z39.48-1992.

Printed in the United States of America

For Ted Kluck Sr.
The original snapper, and my best friend.

I miss being twenty-five years old and playing with my friends. Now we're scattered across the country and it's all in the past. If you're lucky enough to experience something that intense when you're young, you pay for it for the rest of your life. —Doug Plank, former Chicago Bear, in *Monsters: The 1985 Chicago Bears and the Wild Heart of Football*

The fear of failure—especially with smart, middle-class white kids—is usually what holds them back, because they are so afraid to screw up. —Tom House, performance psychologist, in *The QB: The Making of Modern Quarterbacks*

CONTENTS

ACKNOWLEDGMENTS

Writing books is fun—but it's even better when you get to make actual, lifelong friends while doing it. At the risk of sounding like the last day of summer camp, this book would not have been possible without long snapper Jon Akemon and former NFL punter Glenn Pakulak. Both relationships quickly transcended "we can help each other" and moved into "we're actually friends who actually care about other, non-football aspects of each other's lives." You guys are both top notch.

There were also a great many cool people who helped with the participatory, immersive aspects of this project. Mike O'Brien, kicker for the Windy City Ravens by night and master's of social work student by day, became a fast friend. Thanks to Petey Corriedo, R. J. Gabaldon, and the rest of the Ravens players and staff for making my one-day contract dream a reality. Special thanks to Justin Snow, Mitch Palmer, and Michael Husted for the warm welcome at the Husted Free Agent Camp in Mobile. Thanks as well to former pro snapper and current snapping coach Kyle Stelter for guiding me through the Mobile process and caring enough to check in on me periodically afterward. Your kindness was noteworthy! Thanks as well to Nolan Owen for the incredibly helpful snapping lesson in Chicago, and to Chris Rubio for the warm welcome, great interview, and access to your Chicago camp last fall.

A huge thanks is also in order for all of the current and former snappers who sat for interviews for this project: Tyler (enjoyed breakfast in Mobile!) and Trever Kruzel, Nate Boyer, Rob Davis, Bryan Pittman, and Tyler Schmitt, as well as snapping agent extraordinaire Kevin

Gold, former NFL special-teams coach Gary Zauner, and man-about-football Terry Shea. I appreciate all of you!

To Union University athletic trainer and professor Jonathan Allen, for helping to get my aging body ready for battle and, more importantly, for thinking this was cool. And to Christen Karniski, my editor at Rowman & Littlefield, for seeing something in this idea and allowing me to go for it!

To my son, Tristan, for catching snaps; to my dad for catching snaps; and to my son Maxim for the constant positive reinforcement. You guys are a blessing.

Finally, to my darling wife Kristin—you have endured much, and forgiven much, in our time together. My football has taken you to a variety of places—some beautiful and exotic (like France) and most . . . not so much (like Bloomington). Thank you for standing with me in all of it and for the warmth of your embrace after the Bloomington game. Your love and support mean the world. I thank God for you.

INTRODUCTION

Fully Grown Up (Today)

When I was a kid there was a picture hanging in my dad's garage. It was a photograph of his Taylor University offensive linemen—he was their position coach—in their jerseys and military fatigues, sitting menacingly atop a tank that was parked at the Hartford City, Indiana, armory. It was the selfsame tank that my friend Mitch and I would ride our BMX bikes to and enact make-believe childhood military scenarios on. They (the linemen) wore eighties-vintage sunglasses (it was the eighties) and held machine guns. When I was a kid, I could recite their names by heart: James Stamper, Mark Terrell, Randy Brannon, Tim Nordberg, Mike Lee, and some other guys I've forgotten.

For a sport to really hold my gaze, it has to capture me on an aesthetic level. This has only been true of three sports—football, boxing, and cycling. Football and boxing, as I near age forty, are, for obvious reasons, untenable. In a brain-damage-obsessed media culture I can't, in good conscience, continue to pursue sports that will probably damage my brain. As you can imagine, these sports have been a hard habit to break—especially football.

As long as I can remember, I've loved it. My earliest football memory is as a six-year-old, accompanying my dad to practice at the small college near our home. I was completely taken with the eggplant purple helmets, gold pants, and huge shoulder pads. I was drawn to the colors, the bands, and the violence. Sometimes the guys swore. They made me feel a little dangerous, and I liked that feeling. I wanted desperately to be on the inside of their inside jokes. I wanted a jersey. I wanted access to this exclusive club populated with *real men*. In reality, these were small-town kids who were majoring in education, Christian studies, and environmental science. They were going back to Wengatz Hall in the evenings and studying and icing sprained ankles and failing to have the courage to call girls in the same way that I would go back to Wengatz Hall twelve years later, icing my own ankles and having my own courage issues vis-à-vis calling girls.

Still I could, at six, see myself doing this, because it was the closest you could get to being a superhero in real life. Even at six I knew Superman wasn't real, and even if he was, somebody already had the gig.

Now we go to the small college just to walk the dog. It's been years since I was there as a student, and even more years since I played any football there, being that my short career was derailed by some broken bones and an even more broken set of teenaged emotions. The football field is now plastic and painted (in the fashion of all small colleges) with all of the various markings—lacrosse, soccer, and football—that adorn a multi-use field. The stadium was renamed for a local politician who made his money selling cheap fireworks. The dining hall, where I met my wife twenty years ago, has been renovated and barely looks like itself from the outside. The new environmental science building we used to make out behind is now an old building. The bad modern art that adorned the campus when we were there has been removed. There is a building on campus named after my literary agent. Time marches on.

An aside regarding the modern art: There was a statue called "Flexing of Florida" that my feminist English teacher was convinced was totally phallic and that made her not unlike some guys who lived in my dorm who called it "The Morning Erection." There was another sculpture that looked like a giant black dog turd.

As is often the case, Dad and I end up talking about Taylor football. He tells me about the guys in the picture. One of them is dead. Others have had troubles of various kinds—not related to football but totally related to just growing up and being an adult and being alive. I sympathize and relate. For the first time in a year and a half, I don't snap a football to my father.

❊ ❊ ❊

Today I am living, for the first time in decades, in a postfootball life, and ironically, I'm still in colorful tights. On my way back from my last arena football game a few weeks ago, I purchased (impulse-control issues?) a vintage 1981 Motobecane French racing bicycle with a lugged, steel frame and old-school down-tube shifters. It's so old the brake cables are outside the handlebar wrap. On the same day I ordered a set of cycling tights that, in any other context, would be ridiculous and may be, even in this context, still ridiculous. They are blue and yellow and adorned with the logos and company names of a handful of European business interests. I will be hard to miss, road wise, in these tights, as I will look like a giant pedaling lemon. They came with a tag indicating that they are "officially licensed" Tour de France tights.

Two years ago I lived and played football in France. I flew into the Charles de Gaulle Airport in Paris with my wife and two kids, and from there we took a train and midnight car ride to a little stone cottage in the countryside. The cottage was from the sixteenth century. Back then it was a haven for fishermen who came to Brittany to work the English Channel. For two months it was a haven for an aging American football player and coach with a serious yen for adventure.

I played in a game, in Normandy, two days later against a superior team. I got a concussion and a broken rib. I had more fun than I'd had in years. Half my teammates smoked cigarettes before, during, and after the game. We shared a case of beer on the bus ride home, and the guys were, to a man, incredibly gracious and kind to my wife and sons for the duration of our stay.

I didn't snap a football. I didn't even tell the team that I was a snapper, because I just didn't want to deal with the pressure. I made friends with an oral surgeon named Clement, who moonlit as our team's best wide receiver. He was a vintage bike enthusiast and helped me find my Motobecane.

"Come back and ride Paris-Brest-Paris with me!" he e-mails. Clement has the tall, willowy, no-body-fat physique of the competitive cyclist. I have the thick physique of an aging linebacker—not exactly fat, and still athletic, but just *thick*—the sort of thick that makes you feel you're hauling around a trailer full of bricks when pedaling a bike. "So, you're gonna take off some of the weight now that you're cycling?" my dad asks, on a recent phone call. "You're hauling a lot of extra weight around." Thanks, Pops. I'm sure he doesn't mean to make me feel horrible about my physique, and perhaps he's going through the thing that happens to old men where they completely lose their filter and start saying things out loud that shouldn't be said out loud.

"I look like Mr. Incredible before he got in shape," I say, dejectedly, to my wife while looking in the mirror and wearing the lemon tights.

I would love to go back to France and ride Paris-Brest-Paris with Clem, but the fact of the matter is that cycling is a new and tenuous part of my detox from a lifetime of football addiction. It is my halfway house—a sport meant to help gently usher me off the field and back into some semblance of a normal, healthy lifestyle that doesn't involve shopping for helmets on eBay and playing in semi-pro games. That said, I don't want to squeeze the life and the hope out of it by going too far too fast. It's kind of like a new relationship with a girl I like and who, I think, might like me.

The NFL news cycle grinds on through early spring, for the first time without my rapt attention. Pro days are being held, forty times are recorded, NFL draft rumors are bandied about, and I don't care. This is what it feels like to not care. This is what it feels like to not check your phone several times a day for free agency and draft updates. There is a familiar and comforting constancy to the noise, but there's also the sense that guys like Adam Schefter—who have multiple cellular devices and have devoted their lives to "breaking" NFL news—must on some days wake up to what feels like a black, empty existential crisis when they realize that they are getting older, grayer, and progressively less magnificent while the subjects of their life's work, the athletes, remain young and radiant, swathed in the latest and most garish spandex-infused fashions Nike can muster.

Re: the athletes. There is also a curious anonymity, even for the more famous ones. There's the sense that in 2016, I've forgotten the names of most of the guys who were in the 2010 NFL draft. I couldn't tell you what happened in the 2010 free agency period because it is, in a sense, the cheapest and most disposable type of consumable entertainment. The athletes are just the grist in the mill—just the muscle that keeps the programming engine rolling.

The long snapper is the most anonymous player in this entire, annual theater production. Even the kickers—they of the weird facemasks and soccer backgrounds—get more column space during the off-season than snappers. The reality is that major-college football graduates hundreds of snappers each year, but in a given off-season there may only be (due to retirement or injury) one or two "available" NFL snapping jobs. It is the longest of long shots, which makes it super sad but also super interesting. At any given time there are hundreds of guys pursuing the single, open job with a monk's sense of devotion—snapping in empty high school gyms before work in the morning and driving to area gyms to move weights around amidst "regular" people such as teachers, bankers, and insurance salesmen who have knocked off early after a boring day at the office.

This book is devoted to those guys and to the telling of their stories. There is an entire industry out there predicated on the selling and nurturing of "the Dream," and there are various people—coaches, agents, and players—at various levels of this industry. This book is about the Dream and is equal parts a respectful meditation on it and a gentle critique of it. It acknowledges both that the Dream is totally worth pursuing and that there's something noble about the dogged pursuit; but there is also an acknowledgment that in no cases explored in this book is the Dream ultimately satisfying.

When I was six, gazing at NFL magazines and the Taylor football picture on the wall, I thought somehow that it all held the key to ultimate satisfaction. If I could just one day snap in *one* NFL game or play for *one* season, then the rest of my life would be filled with banquets in my honor, I'd be asked to speak at Blackford High School's graduation,[1] and I would be respected and honored everywhere I went. I would have a bunch of memories to reflect on, wistfully. I would know people who had done things that mattered, and in fact, I would have done something that *mattered*. I would have thrown a ball fifteen yards between my legs in a game that was on television. It was going to be beautiful.

I pursued it with a freakish determination. I lifted and ran while my friends partied. I was markedly more religious about it than I was about my actual religion. Regarding religion: I thought God "owed" it to me for a while, because I had grown up on a steady diet of shallow "I trusted God and then I made it to the NFL" narratives. And then I experienced what it felt like to not be good enough—a feeling that is real and relatable for most people, regardless of whatever very special dream it is that they nurture. I wasn't good enough. I wasn't special. I wasn't going to be the guy in the magazine "giving all the glory to the Lord." I was going to be, like most people, anonymous.

My wife entered this hurricane of dysfunction when we were both young. She encouraged me to read and write. I did. In the intervening years I wrote twenty books, all of which reside on a continuum that tops out at "pretty successful" (foreign-language releases, awards, and multiple printings) and on the other end of which is "sold six copies." None of this held a candle to the thrill of being a football player, which is why, eighteen months ago, I started snapping again.

Now I'm in the strange position, teaching college kids to write, of both nurturing their dreams and gently encouraging them not to place all of their psychic eggs in one basket. And to realize that sometimes the worst thing about having dreams is living them.

☆ ☆ ☆

Today, I bike. I do love the aesthetics of this sport: the simple engineering of the bike and the gentle, nearly silent rattle of chain over hub. The skinny tires make a nice hum as they glide over pavement. I can see my shadow and notice that my pedal stroke isn't nearly as circular and beautiful as that of a pro cyclist. I can't go very far. In Tennessee the bicycling is hilly and challenging—there are no flats—you're always either climbing or descending. You're always shifting.

I don't look good enough to wear the tight cycling jersey yet. My compromise is the shorts, with a loose Nike Dri-Fit covering my upper body. As I push up a steep hill, I am exploring the outside edges of my endurance limits. I feel a searing in my lungs and legs, as the legs fill up with lactic acid. I smell the wild chives, which are indigenous to West Tennessee.

I am alone but not lonely. It will be a while before I do this with anybody, as I have too much business to do with my own endurance first.

I haven't snapped a football in three weeks. I no longer dream of football. But what's scarier, maybe, is that I no longer dream of anything. This is, perhaps, what it feels like to be fully grown up.

I

WALKING ON BROKEN GLASS

I heard the sound first. It sounded like glass breaking in the movies, except that it was glass breaking in my basement. It was the front edge of a long winter in Michigan, and I had just started snapping again. I enlisted my twelve-year-old son, Tristan, to kneel seven yards back, as a holder, and catch my practice snaps. Tristan is a good athlete, but I had forgotten or underestimated the speed at which a good snap rockets back toward the holder. I settled over the ball, sitting on a piece of remnant basement carpet in an otherwise sleepy, taupe suburb. I was the only guy in the "Village Place" development practicing long snapping in his basement on a November evening.

The ball went through a plate-glass window in my basement and, rather than shattering the window, just put a bullet-type hole in it . . . if the "bullet" in question was a regulation NFL game ball (circa Pete Rozelle). I felt the cold breeze immediately, and then the first snow of the season began to fall into the window. Shards of glass littered the basement floor. "Figures," I said. I've always had a contentious relationship with Michigan weather in that I, irrationally, take it personally.

"Are you mad at me?" Tristan asked. He felt really sheepish. Usually when stuff like this happens around the house, it's his fault. Tonight, the blame is all on me.

"No buddy; that was my fault. All me." I would take the fall for this because it was entirely my fault. It was my fault for being a dumbass in his late thirties who thought he could snap his way back into pro football after snapping (poorly) his way out of it nearly a decade before.

Hanging on the wall near the window are a bunch of jerseys I wore in games and years past. The irony and sadness of this is not lost on me.

Tristan had a look on his face suggesting that he wanted more proof. Specifically, he wanted to know how I was going to spin this when Mom arrived home. The phone blew up with Mom's distinctive ring tone (NFL Films, "The Autumn Wind"). "Hey, Baby," I said. "Hey . . . what's wrong?" she asked. Women have a way of knowing within a few words that something is wrong. It's a tone-of-voice thing.

She thought that one of the boys had busted their face open on my watch and that we were on our way to the ER. I realized that a little mystery-building silence would actually help me in this situation, so I played it for maximum effect.

"Nobody's hurt," I said finally. "But I broke a window in the basement . . . long snapping."

There was a long silence on the other end of the line.

She finally laughed a little and said she was on her way home. This was a best-case scenario. I immediately shifted my attention to the hole in the window. I called my buddy Eric, a builder, and revealed that I had no idea what to do. He was more interested in *how* the window broke. I told him I broke it long snapping. "You mean it wasn't Tristan?" he asked. "Dude, you were snapping footballs? That is *so* cool! Are you gonna play again?"

✿ ✿ ✿

I am a long snapper. This is to say, I have spent a great deal of my football life bent over a football, with a guy either kneeling seven yards behind me or standing at fifteen yards. My job is to fire a perfect spiral, as fast as I can, at my target, and then embark on a few seconds that fits, on a continuum, between "blocking and tackling" and "trying not to get killed." I snapped professionally in a low-rent arena league for $250 per game. The best of the best, in the NFL, can command almost a million dollars a year to do it.

As a long snapper, you have one job—to go unnoticed. If people get up to get a beer or go to the bathroom during your play, and then nothing noteworthy happens and they don't even know they missed you, then you've done your job. However, it's also a job in which flubbing a snap can mean instant unemployment.

I learned this the hard way when, after snapping (mostly) successfully my entire career, I began inexplicably skipping balls back to the holder. I lost my job, and even though I played in semi-pro leagues and in Europe afterward, I never snapped a football again.

Until now.

This book will explore the art and the craft of long snapping from the perspective of a former snapper trying—for my own edification—to perfect what is imperfect. Simply put, I want to be able to snap perfectly again, not because I have dreams of competing at the highest level (I'm too old) but simply to "right" an old "wrong."

I will enlist the help of boutique snapping superagent (is this a thing?) Kevin Gold and a variety of current and former snappers to help me on my journey. The story will culminate in one *last* pressure-packed situation, as I snap for pro scouts in a pro tryout scenario and then, hopefully, in a game.

❊ ❊ ❊

I took apart a cardboard box and used half a roll of duct tape taping it over the hole in the window, which is what Eric said to do. My kids stood nervous and slack jawed as I taped, racing against the snow. This was something different for Dad to be doing, and I could tell it really entertained them. It was surprisingly airtight, and for a moment I stopped feeling like an idiot for snapping and started feeling pleased at how I fixed the hole.

I called my dad on the way to Home Depot. "Pops," I said. "I broke a window in the basement . . . working on my long snapping." He laughed and, I could tell, turned away from the phone for a minute. He was in a car full of people. "T broke a window snapping," I could hear him say. I heard muffled laughter in the background.

Pops snapped at the small-college and semi-pro level back in the late sixties and early seventies. His jerseys hang in my basement, next to mine. It's his fault that I became a snapper. I blame him. Unlike much of my generation, I can't blame him for being distant, cold, uninvolved, or unfaithful to my mom. He was none of those things. He was a great father.

I was probably in grade school when I first bent over a ball and fired it back to him. The snaps were tight spirals and then, with practice, they became lasers. It was one of the few things I did for my father that I could tell made him actually and visibly proud. "You could do this on Sundays," he said, at one point. It was maybe the happiest moment of my athletic life.

In spite of a nasty case of athletic anxiety, I got pretty good and had big dreams. I remember a recruiting visit to Indiana, in which Pop and I were shown the facility by a graduate assistant (Mark Hagen) and then ushered into a theater to watch the Indiana highlight film on a wall-sized screen. I went home on cloud nine. By God, I would be somebody.

❊ ❊ ❊

Jon Akemon and I played in the same middle-of-nowhere-Indiana, small-college conference, albeit in vastly different eras. Jon was a defensive end and long snapper for the tiny Anderson University Ravens in the late 2000s. When I played for also-tiny Taylor University in the midnineties, hair metal was on its way out (even in Indiana) and Kurt Cobain had just died. And I had just decided that I no longer wanted to be a long snapper. I didn't want the pressure of bending over a ball with beat-up hands, and I didn't want the pressure of a special-teams coach standing over me in practice, yelling at me to "Get it up!" if it's low, and "Keep it down!" if the snap is too high. This is what qualified, in the midnineties, as "coaching" a long snapper.

I didn't want to feel the slick exterior of a balloon-like practice ball ever again. I didn't want to check the weather and wonder how it would affect my snapping. I didn't want the nervous, sick feeling that I would get on third down, knowing that I'd soon have to snap on fourth down. "Punt team! Get hot!" the coach would shout.

Sadly, a perfect drive was one that ended in a touchdown and a two-point conversion. The next-best drive was one that stalled at the opponent's thirty—too close for a punt and too far for a field goal. I was a good snapper but a nervous wreck. To say that I didn't have the disposition for the position would be a massive understatement. I had my father's gift for snapping but my mother's high-strung and nervous disposition. And I had the thinker's curse—I thought a lot . . . about everything. It has helped me tremendously as a writer but has generally ruined me as a football player.

I spent an inordinate amount of time wondering how my teammates and coaches perceived me, wondering if they noticed my effort, and wondering if I intimidated them (good) or if they noticed that I was trying to play college football in a perpetual state of anxiety and disappointment (and the fact that I wasn't as good as I thought and wasn't having any fun). I thought about my coaches. I wondered if they were happy. I wondered if they were dicks at home too, or if it was just a persona they affected for the benefit of the team. I wondered if their wives loved them. I wondered how hot it would be for the afternoon practice. I wondered if the rain would soften the concrete-like practice field. There was always something to think about, besides what I should have been thinking about, which was nothing much at all.

My sense is that Jon Akemon just loved playing football and did so without the aforementioned dilemmas, over a decade later when he flung footballs between his legs for the Anderson Ravens. Akemon has a distinctly southern Indiana drawl, hailing from just north of Louisville. It is the accent of the middle-of-nowhere mid-South. Not quite Louisville (which is its own distinct thing) and not quite backwoods Kentucky. He has a receding hairline, though he is over a decade younger than me, and because I am vain and shallow, this makes me feel better. He's also a great snapper.

Akemon spent a solitary, blessed minicamp as a member of the Tennessee Titans. He has been hungry to reenter the NFL ever since. There was a jersey in a locker in an NFL facility with his last name on the back. There was an upscale hotel-room key in his pocket, courtesy of said NFL team. He boarded a bus at the hotel each morning, bound for a facility that had the best of everything. He hung out with first-round draft choices. It was a charmed, if temporary, existence. Now he snaps, waits for the phone to ring, and advises a writer.

"You need to get some snaps on film if I'm going to help you," he explains. I knew this would have to happen at some point, and even the thought of snapping for a camera makes me nervous. This doesn't bode well for my hopes of snapping for a real team in front of real people again. But my snaps *are* getting better. After retiring my son as a holder and fixing my basement window, I made a new target and snapped at it every day. The target was a folding chair with an orange end-zone pylon on top of it. My goal was to knock off the pylon.

I would snap in the morning, in my pajamas, before work. I would snap after returning from the freshman comp classes I taught at a local college. I would carefully remove my wedding ring and fold up my glasses—taking off the vestiges of manhood so that I could return to being a boy. "You gonna snap some balls, Dad?" my nine-year-old would ask. He knew my routine.

I would spit on my fingers and then settle over the ball, firing it back at the pylon, night after night, ball after ball. Finally, I worked up the courage to ask one of my students—a college baseball player—to catch some snaps for me on film, after class. We planned to snap and film on the baseball team's gleaming, new FieldTurf surface, except that we were in the midst of a full-on Michigan thunderstorm, complete with hail and a side of sleet. After class cleared out, I moved some desks and cleared a seven-yard path in the middle of the room. I hurried to the faculty bathroom and changed into a pair of UnderArmour sweats and a T-shirt.

I chose the baseball player because he was a nontraditional—an older senior with a year of eligibility who wanted to use it to play college football someplace else. He had dreams too. I paced out seven yards on the institutional classroom carpet. And I started to snap. The snaps hit his hands with a satisfying thwack. A couple of girls stayed behind to work on their papers. They couldn't have cared less about what their professor was doing, a few paces away. "I wish I was good at sports," one of them, a vocal-performance major, said. "I wish I was good at singing," I replied, before firing another snap. A soccer player stood on a chair and filmed on his iPhone.

Akemon said I needed ten good ones in a row, no editing. And I was surprised at how fast they came, one after another. It was easier snapping at an adult target than at the orange pylon in my basement.

When I watched the film clips I was most surprised at the sound. Whoosh, thunk. Whoosh, thunk. My snaps sounded like little jet planes.

✦ ✦ ✦

Akemon was coy about his own snapping future. He snapped successfully in a small, start-up pro league called the Fall Experimental Football League (FXFL). The league was the brainchild of a former Ole Miss football player and current New York City businessman named

Brian Woods. The league had four teams, and Akemon played for an outfit called the Brooklyn Bolts who played in a minor league baseball stadium in the hipster capital of the world. He was named to the All-FXFL team as a snapper.

The league boasted some truly big names—former NFL standout Tim Hightower and former Clemson star Tajh Boyd were the league's headliners. Rosters were populated with lots of young guys who were NFL camp casualties. The football was good, but it took place largely in front of empty stands in places such as Omaha, Nebraska, and Boston, Massachusetts. They were empty because nobody really knew it existed. I found out after the fact.

"We all had our training camps in Omaha, Nebraska," explained Boston Brawlers head coach Terry Shea. Shea has an impressive resume including stints as the head coach at Rutgers and offensive coordinator of the Chicago Bears. "And then we would fly to our respective cities for the games. One team, the Blacktips, didn't have a home stadium." The league was an interesting and winsome mix of both legitimacy and thrown-togetherness. Shea—always polite and curious about my projects—listens carefully as I explain the snapping book concept. "We could have you in for a George Plimpton experience!" he says.[1] I don't have the heart to ask him to clarify how serious he is about that. I decide, for the time being, to just be hopeful.

"I would grab a teammate and just take a train into the city and walk around," Akemon said. I imagined the thickly muscled men walking around Brooklyn in their sweatsuits, past vintage T-shirt shops, beards, Red Wing boots, and pretentious bistros, wishing someone would ask them if they played pro football.

And as soon as the season began, it was over again. Each team played only a handful of games, and afterward the players dispersed and began to wait.

I decided to write to Woods about my crazy experiment, in the hopes that he'd give me a shot:

Hello Brian,

My name is Ted Kluck, and I'm an award-winning, internationally published author of over a dozen books. My journalism has appeared on ESPN.com, in *ESPN the Mag*, and many other outlets.

I'm writing because I've signed a contract with Rowman & Littlefield Publishing to write the definitive book on . . . long snapping. That's not a typo. Anyway, I've played and coached my whole life (HS, small college, semi-pro, Europe) and have snapped most of my life. My last in-game snapping experience was in an indoor league in 2006, and I inexplicably snapped horribly. So this book is, in part, a memoir of me trying to get my snapping right and then snapping successfully one more time in a game. That's where you and the FXFL (potentially) come in.

I'm working with some pro snappers (Jon Akemon, Justin Snow) and getting better . . . but I need a last competitive snapping experience. I spoke to Terry Shea about this—as he's been a huge help on some of my past books—and he mentioned that it might be cool to have a "George Plimpton type" embedded experience in a training camp. Admittedly, I don't know how serious he was about this! That said . . . it could be as short as a few days . . . perhaps as long as a few weeks. Just a chance to snap in a scrimmage or "live" situation.

I know it's a crazy idea . . . but it would be cool documentation in a book for your team/league, and it would be something I'd highlight in my other media (blog, podcasts, etc.), which would provide some exposure for the league. I'm fascinated by the development of your league, and feel like it would make a great side-story line.

My particulars are below, and I have tape available if you're interested. Thanks so much for even considering this!

Best,
Ted Kluck
Ht: 6'2"
Wt: 244
Age (cringe): 39

Teams/Leagues:
Blackford (IN) HS
Taylor University
Battle Creek Crunch (CIFL)
St. Brieuc Licornes (France)
Many semi-pro clubs

* * *

One of the realities of life as a self-employed writer is the constancy of worry about things like income, bill paying, and health insurance. Because of the latter, I have taken a part-time job in the wee hours of the morning unloading a jet airplane for UPS. Each morning I awake at 4:20 a.m., throw on some work clothes and a bright yellow vest, and make the solitary coffee-guzzling drive out to UPS. In the winter I often make this drive through snow and freezing rain. I can get almost an entire thermos of coffee down during the fifteen-minute drive. It is less an exercise in pleasure and more about getting caffeine into my body in order to wake it up.

I then trudge into the guard shack, where I'm greeted by a preternaturally cheerful older guy named Rohinton, who is a die-hard fan of the Florida Gators. "Hey, Chief," he says. "Think Tebow is going to make a roster this year?" Rohinton is your classic Tim Tebow apologist and evangelist. I don't have a dog in the Tebow fight, but I enjoy bantering with Rohinton.

I don't have the time or, frankly, the inclination to tell him that I once spent a day in a Mobile, Alabama, hotel suite with Team Tebow, as the quarterback was the main attraction at the Senior Bowl all-star game. I neglect to tell him that I was a finalist to ghostwrite Tebow's "autobiography"—an exercise that almost certainly would have been miserable (because of the level of family-related "crazy" I observed in the hotel room) but also, almost certainly, would have made me the kind of rich man who didn't have to work at UPS in the morning to get health insurance.

"He's a good runner, Boss," I say, in response, as cheerfully as I can at that hour.

From there, I swipe a time card, something I haven't done since college. We are then led through a series of stretches—eerily similar to being an athlete—because the off-loading of all that freight is a strenuous activity.

I work on "top deck," meaning that I ride a piece of machinery twenty feet into the air in order to climb inside the plane with a crew of two other guys so that we can pull four-thousand-pound "cans" out of the plane. I'm reminded of the kinds of things I used to do to train for football in college, things like pulling heavy, weighted sleds and pushing my car up and down Greenwood Drive, back in Hartford City. This is like a paid version of that. The shift is usually over and done with in the span of about two hours.

My work at UPS takes place in a sort of strange semi-life in that we come and go in the dark and rarely if ever see each other in "real life." I learn that most of my coworkers are entrepreneurs—financial planners, lawyers, real-estate investors, landscapers, and builders. They're all in it for the health insurance.

I'm doing things on this job like wearing an orange vest and lifting with my legs and not with my back. There are many more ways to be injured or killed while doing this job, making it, in some ways, a lot more stressful than sitting at a computer. There's a surprising amount of mental work that goes into not getting injured/killed, dispelling the myth that most blue-collar work is mindless.

Essentially I'm getting paid to use my body and my mind, instead of just my mind. And while the work has been difficult in some ways, God has blessed me through it in many others.

The worst thing I could possibly do here is write some egghead/nerd piece that tries to intellectualize physical labor or otherwise romanticize it in a literary way. That would be dumb and patronizing and also probably not all that surprising. As every pro athlete everywhere would say, it (physical labor) "is what it is."

Sometimes when I tell people what I'm doing, they react as though I've just told them that I've been diagnosed with a terminal disease. "Oh, Ted," said one friend. Sometimes they put a hand on my shoulder, concernedly, as they say these things. I do appreciate the concern, but the thing is, I really like this job. In some ways I like it better than writing.

Not surprisingly, working on this kind of job site has given me an appreciation for guys who do this labor full time and have done so their whole lives. It's hard on the body, mind, and soul, albeit in different ways than deskwork.

Speaking from experience as a working writer, critiques from readers/constituents can be especially vicious. These critiques tend to be of the "I feel called to tell you how much I hate your ideas" variety, with the occasional "and incidentally I also think you're a jerk, personally." For some of us (read: me), this criticism is really hard to take. It's one of the worst parts of being an author (along with editorial interactions in which editors generally mean well and are helpful but are still tinkering with my words, which is its own kind of misery).

At my blue-collar job, the critiques tend to be more of the "move out of the way so you don't get hit by this piece of machinery" variety, which is helpful, immediate, and beneficial in that it keeps me alive. It's perfunctory and completely impersonal. I find that I really appreciate the lack of emotion in my blue-collar job.

Another consolation, believe it or not, is waking up well before dawn. I thought this would be brutal, but it really isn't. I enjoy the quiet house and the predawn calm. A lifelong insomniac, I'm now so exhausted at night that I rarely have trouble falling asleep. This is another consolation that sounds small but to an insomniac is extremely significant.

Coming from a sedentary writing career for the last decade, I've been relentless in my pursuit of a "life of the body," which has included forays into the following: boxing, semi-pro football (repeatedly), softball, track and field, church basketball, and even professional wrestling. Most of these pursuits (at least the football and boxing) were a means of proving that I was not "soft" even though I thought/wrote for a living.

My job provides a level of physical challenge and danger that satisfies many of the longings I sought for so many years as a competitive athlete. And the people who do work this kind of work tend to be tough and tend not to whine and complain. This is a quality that I'd like to cultivate in myself and that I admire in people who have it.

And it gives me plenty of time to think about snapping.

2

KEVIN GOLD

Agent to the Anonymous

"How's your snapping?" is the first thing out of agent Kevin Gold's mouth. I laugh. I don't get asked that much these days. But he listens intently as I talk about the intricacies of firing snaps against my base-ment wall. He is either actually interested or very good at faking it.

"My phone doesn't ring at two in the morning," explains premiere agent-to-the-nonstars Kevin Gold, when I ask him why he'd rather rep-resent long snappers than players at more glamorous positions. "Long snappers tend to be humble, steady, reliable, and low-maintenance people," he explains.

Sports representation has been both glamorized and vilified in me-dia and pop culture, but it is often the agent who gets the middle-of-the-night call when the athlete has gotten into trouble or needs money. And stories abound of the lengths to which prospective agents will go to secure a client. None of this, apparently, is a factor for Gold, who still practices law during the day but has created for himself a niche of a niche of a niche with his boutique long-snapping agency.

I first saw *Jerry Maguire* on my honeymoon. At the time I was twenty years old, only a year or so removed from the heartbreak of an injury-shortened college career. I was madly in love with my wife and, like all new husbands, had a head full of dreams as to what the future would look like, which (at twenty) probably looked like a life full of sex and awesomeness. But the youthful swagger matched a gnawing heartache over the feeling that I had left football "stones" unturned. I was bitter about the end of my career and already looking for a way to get back onto the field. I needed to compete and, at twenty, was convinced I had something left.

Maguire was the perfect film in that it "scratched" several concurrent itches: it not only captured my imagination as a young writer but also fed the desire for football. For me, it was a two-hour orgy of contracts, negotiations, minicamps, helmets, equipment, the NFL draft, and everything else I'd ever dreamed of. "It's not show friends; it's show business," said the douche villain Jay Mohr character, Bob Sugar. I loved it.

Shortly after the ill-fated *Maguire* viewing, I drove several hours to Nashville for a cattle-call open tryout with the now-defunct Nashville Kats of the Arena Football League (AFL). It was miserable in that there were several hundred guys there competing for, realistically, probably zero jobs in that these cattle calls are more about local marketing and the fifty-dollar entry fee than they are about any tangible opportunities. It was my first brush with the reality that there are entire industries that trade upon the fragile dreams of young people. To have the dream is one thing, but it's another thing entirely when you begin shelling out money for it.

Nashville's coach stood on a corner of AstroTurf and chomped on an unlit cigar. If Hollywood's central casting came up with a rendering of "grizzled football coach," it would have been this guy. I drove home a few hours later with a sprained ankle, a bad tape job (see ankle), a gash on my forehead from a one-on-one drill, my fifty-dollar T-shirt, and no AFL contract.

"There's something about this job, snapping, that makes people think they can do it," Gold says.

> I get e-mails from guys who are thirty-two years old, five foot nine, and 260 pounds, who have never played organized football, but think they can snap in the NFL. But it's an incredibly difficult and unlikely job. There are only thirty-two of these jobs in the world, and most of them, at any given time, are occupied by people who are very good at what they do and who will be there for a long time. I tell people it's like being elected president. It's that rare.

Still, there is nothing jaded or "grizzled" about Gold's demeanor, and he is a savvy enough communicator to know not to crush his interviewer's modest dreams. "Keep at it!" he implores. At the same time, he acknowledges that the landscape has changed. Rags-to-riches long-snapping stories are fewer and farther between now that snapping has become a cottage industry, and now that there are boutique tutors and websites devoted to securing scholarships for players who specialize in the art of firing a ball through their legs.

"You wouldn't believe some of the e-mails I get from parents," he says. "Last year at one of [Chris] Rubio's camps, an eighth-grader was offered [a college scholarship]. I think it was more of a PR thing, but still."

It is a feeding frenzy. College football has never been more glamorous and overexposed, and a college education has never been more expensive. The result is an environment in which parents are encouraged to be openly maniacal and careerist about their early adolescents in all sports. And the result of that is a football environment where someone like Chris Rubio can flourish. Rubio, a former college long snapper, has positioned himself as the marquee shaper and marketer of long-snapping talent in the country. He has done this largely on the power of his social media presence and a series of camps, where attendees are promised an opportunity to snap under the watchful eye of college scouts (via Rubio's video archiving and ranking). On that front, Rubio delivers. I make a mental note to contact Rubio and see the feeding frenzy in person. It promises to be interesting.

Gold's own online presence started more modestly but with no less impact. "In the late nineties, right after Al Gore invented the Internet, I started a weird little website aimed at putting a face on the guys who do this anonymous job week after week," he explained. "It was kind of a whim, because in the late nineties, everybody thought that starting a website was the thing to do." The website was Longsnap.com, and I remember finding it myself in the early 2000s when I was toiling in obscurity as a semi-pro long snapper. I thought it was the coolest thing ever. Longsnap.com told the unique "road to the NFL" stories of long snappers and also archived the signings, releases, and trades involving NFL snappers. "Yeah, some people thought it was the coolest thing ever," says Gold. "Like, 'Wow, there's a whole website devoted to long snapping!' Other people thought it was a sign of the apocalypse because . . . it was a whole website devoted to long snapping."

* * *

Gold went to law school at Widener, where like many young lawyers he had dreams of becoming a sports agent. "I had a couple of small-school clients at Shippensburg University," he recalls. "But a friend of mine said, 'You should talk to Rob Davis.' Davis was a decent Division II lineman but, as you know, decent Division II defensive linemen don't make it in the NFL."

Davis had been signed as an undrafted free agent by the New York Jets but failed to make the roster. He and his initial agent had lost touch. "I agreed to meet Rob at a mall food court, of all the glamorous places," says Gold. "He said, 'I want to try to make it as a long snapper.'"

At the time, the Canadian Football League (CFL) was experimenting with teams in the United States. Davis signed with the Baltimore Stallions franchise and won a Grey Cup—the CFL's version of the Super Bowl. He was then signed and cut by the Kansas City Chiefs, and snapped for a season for the Chicago Bears before settling in as Green Bay's starting snapper from 1997 to 2007. "For two or three years, Rob and I had the *Jerry Maguire*–type story," says Gold. "He was my only client."

Maguire, in the movie, had but one lonely client, Rod Tidwell, after Sugar famously fired his mentor at Cronin's. Maguire's bigger-than-life movie persona was modeled on that of real-life superagent Leigh Steinberg. What followed was a sweet story of friendship wrapped in the football movie's standard clothes.

As the profile of Longsnap.com grew, so did Gold's client roster. Unlike Maguire, he didn't really have to recruit, meaning that he didn't have to live through the pride-swallowing siege of crisscrossing the country wooing college students. Gold didn't have to spend hours preparing a slick, book-length recruiting brochure and DVD collection, destined to be tossed into the back of a player's car, never to be flipped through again. The odd genius in Gold's approach is that his "brochure" was already online via a site that glorified a previously anonymous job. "A lot of guys came to me through the website, and I would get a lot of e-mails," he says.

Typically agents are flying around the country attending college games and then waiting patiently by the locker-room door in the hopes of getting five minutes to shove a brochure or DVD into the hands of a prospective client. Often, agents are then expected to shell out sizeable cash "advances" to the athlete, for everything from combine training (legitimate) to walking around money (not so legitimate). At this stage of the game, the athlete knows that he has all the leverage, as most agents are desperate to sign as many clients as possible. Not Gold.

"The big thing now is shelling out ten to fifteen thousand dollars to send a kid to Arizona or Florida so that he can train for the combine and pro days . . . to shave a tenth of a second off his forty-yard dash time," says Gold. "With snappers, it's different. That stuff doesn't matter nearly as much. Occasionally I'll pay for a client to be able to work with Justin [Snow] to perfect the snapping element."

Justin Snow would become Gold's second client. Snow was an undersized, underwhelming defensive end in a then under-the-radar college program (Baylor) when he decided to mess around with long snapping at Baylor's pro day. He wasn't even Baylor's starting long snapper in college.

"Chris Polian, from the Indianapolis Colts, saw Justin snapping and said, 'Son, you can be an NFL long snapper,'" Gold recalls. Snow was invited to camp and, against all odds, won the job. It was a job he held onto for twelve seasons as one of the NFL's most consistent snappers.

"I think he only screwed up one snap in his entire career," Gold recalls: "in the snow against New England. At the NFL level it becomes entirely mental, and Justin always told me to watch the next snap right after the bad one. That will reveal the rest of the guy's career. His next snap was perfect."

Stories abound of guys who, for one reason or another, just "lose it" mentally. This was my experience. What was once a rote, mindless, muscle-memory activity became, for me, an occasion for over-thought and obsession. Snapping is, in some ways, the ultimate perfectionist's activity, because perfection is actually attainable in snapping in a way that it isn't in writing, where the combination of words and ideas holds infinite possibilities for improvement. Either snaps are fast and accurate or they aren't. But for the perfectionist who is suddenly imperfect, the result can be demonically frustrating.

"Who was the guy in Major League Baseball who all of a sudden couldn't throw the ball from shortstop to first? Steve Sax?" Gold wonders. "My guys tell me that if you start thinking about it, you're done."

I have been spending hours in the basement working on the physical act of snapping, but perhaps what I really need to work on is not thinking about it. This will prove to be much more difficult.

"There was a guy named Ryan Pontbriand on the Cleveland Browns who is still the highest-drafted snapper in history," says Gold. Pontbriand was drafted in the fifth round by the Browns. "He had a great career for four to five seasons and then the wheels just came off. I've had Packers long snappers for almost two decades, since Rob Davis. These are guys who don't think about it. It's the same football, and the same motion, every time."

"It was one of those hard things to know whether to talk about it or not talk about it," Browns kicker Phil Dawson told Cleveland.com upon Pontbriand's release. "You could tell he was aware of the issues. He did everything he could to fix it. Snapping hundreds of balls. Snapping at home. Watching film. For whatever reason, it didn't work itself out."

"It's hard to explain," Gold said in the same article. "I ask my guys about this all the time. If you rebound from one bad snap, then it's not an issue. Some guys rebound, and some let it get to them. It becomes a mental issue. Then you're double-clutching and triple-clutching. Once that happens, you're done." Pontbriand was a two-time Pro Bowler and was involved in more successful kicks than any other snapper in Cleveland Browns history.

"These are perfectionists," Gold says. "I'll call my guys on Monday afternoons after they've played what I thought was a perfect game. And any little imperfection is, for them, a bad snap."

I ask Gold if he still gets nervous watching his clients snap.

"I get excited/nervous," he says. "I have a client named Bret Goode whose mom has never seen him snap. He played college ball at Arkansas, and is now Green Bay's snapper. Even though she goes to almost every game, she turns away and puts her head in her hands every time he snaps. She can't watch."

Her response is an interesting unintended commentary on the idolatry of pro football. In reality, her son flubbing a snap would be, at worst, embarrassing and potentially damaging to his career prospects. But looked at from another angle, it would also be no big deal inasmuch as he is still young, in prime condition, and possessing a college degree that gives him the chance to earn a living in another way. In the pantheon of injury, illness, death, and divorce, throwing the ball over the head of a holder or punter is a completely survivable hard time. I know because I've survived it—not in the NFL, but still. Yet her reaction speaks to the importance of the job and the fact that, from a job-security and visibility standpoint, there is a lot on the line with each snap.

"This is all I do," says Gold. "I'm a specialist *in* the specialists. I know who's good and who's bad. I'm brutally honest [note: I find the 'brutal' part hard to believe]. It's probably the hardest job in the world to get, because there are only one or two openings a year. Guys need to assume that it will take three or four years to get there, like kickers. You have to bounce around the country going to minicamps and trying out. But I can help open the doors.

"I'm not selling 'pie in the sky' here," he says, finally. "There's way more supply than demand."

3

ROB DAVIS

A King's Ransom to Play a Kid's Game

"I don't want a problem with this fucking job," said then Packers head coach Mike Holmgren to his new snapper Rob Davis. "Can you do this fucking job?" Davis dutifully said yes. "Good. Then I'll see you at practice." That was Rob Davis's less-than-warm welcome to a job that he would keep for a long, long time.

Long before he was a Green Bay Packer, though, Davis was cut by his ninth-grade team and was relegated to junior varsity in tenth and eleventh grade. To say that his journey to the league was unlikely would be the most massive of understatements.

"It was my high school coach, Jack Davis, who first said, 'You can probably snap in the NFL.'"

"I was redshirted as a freshman, started playing defensive line, flunked out, came back . . . and then scouts started coming around talking about 'the more you can do.'" Davis started snapping near the end of his college career but still went undrafted and largely unnoticed. "I loaded trucks for a year," he says. "I love the grind. New York Jets scout Pat Kirwan found me working at Town Cleaners and gave me my first opportunity. I still give him a hug every time I see him at the combine."

Davis was cut by the Jets (and then the Chiefs). It was only after a stint in the Canadian Football League (snapping for, weirdly, a franchise based in Baltimore) that Davis had his fateful conversation with

Mike Holmgren and got his opportunity to play with Brett Favre, Reggie White, and the rest of the Green Bay Packers.

Though we routinely celebrate players such as Doug Williams and Shack Harris for breaking the league's color barrier at quarterback, Davis might have been the league's first black long snapper.

"Reggie White couldn't believe it when I walked out to practice for the first time," he says. "He yelled, 'We've got the first black snapper in NFL history!'"

☆ ☆ ☆

Davis is, outwardly, a very confident man—large, black, bearded, and possessing a considerable presence and swagger. Still, he battled fears every time he bent over to snap a football.

"There's a certain fear that exists with it," he says. "Like the old guy with the Red Sox who booted the ball in the World Series [Bill Buckner]. He carries that with him for the rest of his life. I thought about it every Sunday."

It's not news that great athletes make hard things look easy. And I think great athletes also make scary things look not scary. If Davis was wracked with nerves during his career, or besieged by fear, you never knew it. He also managed to be a leader in the locker room, despite being, technically, a specialist.

"You try to be seen and not heard," he explains. "But snappers have a unique standing in the locker room in that they're welcome as a big component of the game but don't present a direct threat to anyone else's position. When the game is on the line in the fourth quarter, the guys are all standing on the sidelines pulling for you, and nobody else wants to make that snap."

Davis also believes that his demeanor and work ethic gave him a measure of acceptance in a legend-laden locker room.

"I was kind of a trendy, East Coast guy, and I was strong in the weight room," he says. "I could talk that street shit. And I could talk on the dark side of the room, if you know what I mean."

I do know what he means. Though race may work better in football than anywhere else in society, there are still natural divisions based on lifestyle and background. But it was his work ethic that gave Davis the greatest measure of acceptance.

"I always tried to make sure Favre knew I was trying my ass off," he says. "I was a scout-team All-American. I went to defensive line and offensive line meetings because I was the emergency player on both sides. I studied film of Chris Doleman and Warren Sapp back then so that I could give the offensive line solid work every day, because back then you were hitting in practice almost every day.

"As a bona fide street hustler I realized I was making a king's ransom to play a kid's game. You've got to fight like an animal for that job. In the NFL you realize that everyone in that locker room has been damn good at every level they've ever played on. You realize that it's harder than you think it is. They're going to give it to you for sixty minutes."

❊ ❊ ❊

On the evening of Rob Davis's last game as an NFL player, the 2007 NFC Championship Game, the wind chill is –23 degrees in Green Bay. Packer Hall of Famer Bart Starr tosses the pregame coin, and living legend Brett Favre buckles his retro-looking Riddell VSR-4 helmet over a head sock designed to keep him warm. Green Bay's linemen, in a show of machismo, refuse to wear sleeves despite the bone-chilling temperatures. "I can't imagine what that feels like," intones Joe Buck.

As the thirty-nine-year-old Davis jogs onto the field to snap for the first time, I appreciate what he must be feeling. At this age, the body rebels each morning and is achy and stiff on the best of days. I can't imagine what it must feel like to perform athletically in these temperatures. I'm also reminded of the sheer amount of *time* and *eras* that Davis has survived as a Packer. He has survived through the Edgar Bennett, Ahman Green, and now Ryan Grant regimes in the Packer backfield. Legendary defensive end Reggie White, who welcomed him onto the Packers, has, in 2007, been dead for three years. When Davis entered the league, television coverage was still relatively low fidelity. Fantasy football was still a small fringe activity. There was no round-the-clock NFL Network and no social media. In 2007, the screen is a gong show of graphics and talking as there is no shortage of story lines and opinions. When Davis entered the league in the midnineties, Troy Aikman was still a player. He is now one of television's favorite talking heads and is a fixture in the Fox booth.

Davis's first punt snap is perfect. He is wearing sleeves.

These were the Brandon Jacobs/Ahmad Bradshaw, ball-control, Eli Manning–minimizing New York Giants. Predictably, they grind away most of the first-quarter clock with a long drive. Being that this is 2007, there is a camera almost permanently affixed to the ruddy and perma-frowned face of Giants coach Tom Coughlin, who seems miserable even under perfect weather conditions. Troy Aikman seems inordinately concerned about frostbite vis-à-vis Coughlin's face.

After a ninety-yard Favre-to-Donald Driver scoring strike in the second quarter, Davis pegs home another perfect snap, in spite of the conditions. Much to the chagrin of kickers, quarterbacks, and receivers, freezing temperatures give the ball a leaden, rocklike feel. It's harder to throw and kick, and it hurts more to catch. It follows that these footballs are harder to snap, as the leather is a little bit slicker and less pliable. And in a profession where grip and dexterity are so important, very few snappers snap with gloves.

The Packers have a safety named Atari Bigby, whose job, it seems, is to tune up Giants receiver Plaxico Burress every time the aforementioned goes near the middle of the field and the football at the same time. He does so repeatedly, with his shoulder and helmet, bouncing Burress painfully off the frozen turf.

Across the field, New York's snapper of the future is rookie Zak DeOssie, of Brown. DeOssie's father, Steve, was a linebacker and long snapper for the Parcells-era Giants, with whom he won Super Bowl XXV. DeOssie was drafted as a linebacker on the strength of a great NFL Combine performance where he ran a 4.58-second forty-yard dash. He took over as the starting snapper after his predecessor, Ryan Kuehl, was placed on injured reserve halfway through the season. The elder DeOssie was a linebacker who snapped, and his son has followed in his footsteps and is, if anything, an oddity because he still logs significant time as a linebacker in this age of specialization.

But tonight DeOssie is on the bench, and his replacement is Penn State defensive lineman Jay Alford, a rookie. He almost recovers a muffed punt in the middle of the second quarter, but his unit would struggle down the stretch.

The story of the game was as one would expect from both teams. Eli Manning didn't lose the game or win it, and Brett Favre was his team's only offense. Ryan Grant rushed for a meager twenty-nine yards, and no other Packer had a positive rush. An unlikely interception-turned-fumble (Favre to R. W. McQuarters to Mark Tauscher) recovery set the Packers up deep in Giants territory in the fourth quarter and allowed Davis's unit to take the field for a game-tying field-goal attempt. Davis's snap is a little to the left, the body side of the holder, but that beats the alternative. It is safely placed, and rookie kicker Mason Crosby successfully converts.

Alford and his unit struggle mightily in this game—a factor leading to a tied score at the end of regulation. In the fourth quarter Lawrence Tynes and the Giants kicking team lines up for a go-ahead field goal. Alford's snap, like Davis's, is safely into the holder's body, though this time the kick sails left.

After another offensive series ends, Alford nervously puts a punt snap on the shoelaces of his punter, who nevertheless pins Green Bay deep in its own territory. It is the kind of snap that goes "in the books" as a good snap but nevertheless keeps the snapper up at night. An inch or two lower, and it skips off the frozen Lambeau Field turf.

Davis drills home a perfect punt snap, deep in his own territory with just over two minutes remaining. It is the dreaded "back to our end-zone" snap that has caused me great anxiety in my career—though Davis drills it.

Green Bay uses its final timeout with four seconds remaining to try to ice Giants kicker Lawrence Tynes. Snapper Alford, bent over the ball, stands back up and must wait another minute to make the snap that could send his team to the Super Bowl. When he is finally able to snap, with the seconds ticking off the clock, Alford's snap is high, and veteran punter Jeff Feagles must stretch his arms skyward to corral it. As a result, Tynes pulls the kick to the left, and the game will go into overtime.

The stentorian Tom Coughlin merely bows his head and puts his hands on his knees as Alford jogs off the field in shame. Green Bay exults in his misfortune as they are still alive, if only for a few moments. Rob Davis joins the other captains at midfield for the overtime coin toss, which the Packers win. A roar goes up from the collected, frozen crowd. Coughlin looks like a candidate for implosion. His face seems to grow ruddier by the second.

Favre, on a bad throw, is intercepted by Corey Webster on the second play of overtime, meaning that, barring a touchdown, Alford and his unit will have a shot at redemption. He takes the field with his unit for a forty-seven-yard field goal to send the New York Giants to the Super Bowl. This time the snap is straight and level: a perfect snap, a perfect hold, and a perfect kick. Manning and Favre share an embrace at midfield, in the kind of moment that makes old athletes look some-how older and grayer. The Giants will journey to Arizona to face New England in Super Bowl XLII. Archie Manning celebrates in his luxury box. The "NFL royalty" story line stays alive for one more week.

DeOssie, New York's heir apparent at long snapper, celebrates with his teammates. Jay Alford, New York's snapper for the moment, is re-deemed for a night, while Rob Davis will never snap in an NFL game again.

Super Bowl XLII is a defensive struggle, and New England leads 7–3 as the fourth quarter begins. It is a surreal watch, even though the game is barely seven years old. One of New England's defensive starters is linebacker Junior Seau who, just a few short years later, would be dead of a supposed concussion-induced suicide. It's chilling to see him colliding all over the field and chilling to see the energy and passion he brought to the Patriot defense.

It is, in many ways, a boring Super Bowl held in a spaceship-esque new stadium in the desert, named cheesily after an online degree mill. In this, it is a glowing example of the modern NFL.

The Giants are customarily unimpressive until they need to be. Al-ford, somewhat shockingly, hangs onto the kick-snapping job through the Super Bowl, though DeOssie takes over punt-snapping duties. His snap is true after Manning's clutch fourth-quarter strike to David Tyr-ee. After a pretty mediocre performance by Manning to that point, the pass is a revelation. It occurs to viewers that this inferior quarterback and his inferior team may in fact slay living legend Tom Brady and the mighty Patriots. It doesn't make sense and will somehow seem wrong if it happens.

Alford snaps well in the game in spite of the fact that he also logs significant reps at defensive tackle—the kind of double duty that snap-pers used to regularly face but that has, in recent years, become almost obsolete at every level. Either way, it is no small thing as a defensive lineman's hands and arms take a beating. Ultimately, the two rookie snappers guide the Giants through the playoffs to an unlikely 17–14 Super Bowl victory.

✵ ✵ ✵

After a long run as Green Bay's only long snapper, Rob Davis was told that he was no longer needed—a reality, he says, that is faced by every NFL player. "I was thirty-nine going on forty, and they said, 'We're going in a different direction.'" Only Brett Favre and Forrest Gregg played in more consecutive games as Packers.

"I didn't make enough to just sit on the couch every day, but I wanted to get out of the pressure cooker," he says.

In 2013 Davis received his master's in applied leadership for teaching and learning at the University of Wisconsin at Green Bay. The topic of his thesis was "At Risk? A Program for Learners at the Middle and Secondary Levels."

Davis has transitioned into a position in the Packer front office as director of player development, in which he does everything from helping players off the field to helping them learn the nuances of getting along in the locker room. He cites Redskins phenomenon-turned-apparent-bust Robert Griffin III as an example of a "bad locker-room look"—specifically Griffin's chummy relationship with team ownership and curious choices like letting his fiancée work out at the team facility. Such things, says Davis, tend to polarize a locker room.

One thing he doesn't do is teach anyone on the team to long snap. "It would be a dick move to teach another one of our players to snap," he explains, given the scarcity of NFL snapping jobs and the unspoken fraternity that exists among snappers. "Our guy [Bret Goode] has been nails. He's gonna drop it in the pocket every time, and if he's gonna miss he's gonna miss low. He's so mentally strong. His stroke is always the same in practice or in a game."

It's the state of today's NFL player that keeps Davis in Green Bay each season. "I'm so heartbroken by some of the things happening around the league," he says. "They're taking this thug shit way too far."

> We just had twenty-five guys in for a tryout weekend and a lot of careers ended this weekend. It takes luck. It takes luck to make it in this league . . . for your body to hold up, and for you to be receptive enough to take it all in. This is an all-star league, and you can be guaranteed that, at some point, they're going to ask you to leave.
>
> I enjoyed being able to live this life from age twenty-three to forty-six. I still believe in the value of hard work and that we should

carry ourselves with a certain amount of pride. I know what these kids are going through because I've been cut four times. I know what it's like to hit the long, lonely highway with tears in your eyes.

4

THE CAUTIONARY TALE

Trey Junkin and the Danger of Living
One Dream Too Many

As a teenage college student playing at small-time Taylor University, I had a *Sports Illustrated* photo of Trey Junkin taped to my dorm-room wall—in part because I still admired long snappers, even though I had, to that point, refused to snap at Taylor. I didn't want the pressure. But I also admired Junkin because he represented the badass ethos I thought I wanted to embody back in the mid-1990s—muscles jacked, sitting atop a Harley Davidson. In reality, it was about as far from "me" as possible. I had no tattoos; I had never ridden a motorcycle. Still, when you're eighteen, trying out personas comes with the territory.

Fast forward to 2002. At age forty-one, long snapper Trey Junkin of the New York Giants was living my present-day dream. It was a sunny afternoon in San Francisco, and Junkin's Giants faced the San Francisco 49ers in the NFC Wild Card game. It was a Giants team with Super Bowl aspirations, led by a rejuvenated Kerry Collins and a flashy, cocky, Miami-educated (heh) tight end named Jeremy Shockey. Junkin had a well-earned rep as one of the league's most consistent snappers, and when he entered the league in 1983 (I was seven), snappers played other positions. Junkin, a fourth-round pick, was a tight end and a linebacker, and actually saw significant tight-end reps as a Los Angeles Raider in the eighties. By the midnineties, Junkin had settled in as a snapping specialist, holding down the position for Seattle and Arizona.

He played sixteen games for the Cardinals in 2001 as a forty-year-old and snapped perfectly in all of them. A fitting end to a long, successful career as one of the league's first snapping specialists.

"He thought that was the perfect opportunity to finally get a ring that after nineteen years had eluded him," Junkin's wife Sarah told the *New York Post*. "He had a lot of confidence and a lot of faith in that team."

In the same piece, Junkin explained that he'd had over 1,700 punt snaps in his career and only two bad ones. He couldn't number the extra point and field-goal snaps but in nearly twenty years had only two botched coming into the game. "Yeah, I think about them," he explained. "I'm a perfectionist."

The 2002 Giants won with a grinding running attack that featured Tiki Barber and a passing game focused almost entirely on Shockey (seventy-four catches) and Amani Toomer (eighty-two). As Junkin bent over the ball in warm-ups, wearing a freshly minted number 48 jersey with his name sewn on, it never occurred to him that he would be remembered for what would unfold over the next three hours, or that he would be remembered at all.

"I never thought about snapping the football while I was on the football field ever," he told the *Post*. "It's just something that I did. It just happened. For the first time in 19 years, I got over a football and started thinking about what I was doing. As soon as I did that, it was over."

Junkin's ability to not think echoes what I've heard from other successful snappers, who just routinely bend over the ball and do something that their muscles have done, on command, for years. Great athletes in any sport have a unique ability to not think in the moment of truth. "It's like a toilet," Junkin told the *Sporting News* on long snapping. "You don't even think about it until it's broken. Then it's a mad scramble to fix it."

Terrell Owens opened the game's scoring by taking a short pass seventy-six yards to the house. It was vintage, prime Owens—using his size and strength to shield and then shake smaller defenders, and then using his speed to explode downfield.

Junkin's afternoon started well, with a perfect snap to punter Matt Allen. "The best thing you can say about Matt Allen as a punter is that he's a good holder," said Joe Buck in what is undoubtedly a line he had practiced for that very moment. But his acclamation of Allen's holding skills would prove to foreshadow kicking game horrors to come.

In the first quarter, Pam Oliver reports on a Jeremy Shockey ice-throwing incident involving some 49er fans. It is a prime example of the overreporting that is rampant in modern NFL media. There are too many story lines, too many angles, and too many people with microphones saying things that don't matter. And this was *before* social media got its narcissistic claws into sports culture. This, incidentally, is the phenomenon that haunts Trey Junkin every year around Wild Card time, as Junkin has (unfairly) become something of a public symbol of failure and shame.

Junkin fires a perfect extra-point snap to end the first quarter and knot the game at seven apiece and then another one just a few minutes into the second quarter after a Shockey touchdown. The narrative that unfolds is a little slice of NFL playoff perfection. There is hatred (of the 49er fans toward Shockey), rivalry (Shockey versus linebacker Julian Peterson), and exemplary performances (Shockey, Toomer, et al.). At this point in the narrative, Junkin isn't even an afterthought. He is what all snappers strive to be—anonymous. He elicits mention for the first time as the second quarter draws to a close, after another perfect snap and after another Giants touchdown.

The Giants take a two-touchdown lead into the halftime locker room, which they will systematically blow through the third and early fourth quarters, setting the scene for the winter (or, more accurately, the fourth quarter) of Junkin's discontent.

With 3:16 remaining in the game, and the Giants in possession of a tenuous 38–33 lead, head coach Jim Fassel elects to kick a field goal instead of going for it on a fourth and one. To go for it, and make it, would have sealed the game for the Giants, who could have then run out the clock. Instead, they line up for a field goal, Junkin fires a snap low and outside, and the kick is shanked. The camera ominously follows Junkin to the sideline where he is shown, from behind, shaking his head. I've been there. It's a miserable feeling, knowing that points have been lost because of your screwup. You want to look into the stands and find your wife while at the same time not wanting her to see you. Junkin was, no doubt, questioning his decision to come out of retirement.

Oddly, there were no teammates consoling Junkin on the film because he was probably largely unknown by his teammates—some of whom were almost young enough to be his children. He would later tell newspaper reporters that he couldn't even find someone on the sidelines to catch practice snaps for him. He was truly a man alone.

The game's denouement is a classic battle of epic, early 2000s football personalities: Terrell Owens battling for yardage in his prime against a league anomaly, white cornerback Jason Sehorn. There is a mud-covered Jeff Garcia scrambling for extra yardage. "Should the Niners come back in this one it would be the second biggest comeback in NFL playoff history," explains Joe Buck. The first biggest being Buffalo's legendary 41–38 comeback victory over Houston in 1993 in a game known simply as "The Comeback."

There is Jeremy Shockey, head bent and hidden under a towel, unable to watch the 49ers chewing up yardage and clock on their way to a Garcia-to-Tai Streets touchdown strike. The game is something of a celebration of the "very good but not great." Garcia and Shockey will not be Hall of Famers, but on this day they made for sensational viewing. Terrell Owens picks up an inevitable unsportsmanlike conduct penalty—inevitable because it is the early 2000s and is a game that Terrell Owens is involved in. The 49ers go for two and don't make it. They lead by one.

On the ensuing possession, Kerry Collins throws a first down strike to Ron Dixon. He hits Dixon again to pick up another first down inside San Francisco's thirty. Kicker Matt Bryant thumps practice kicks into a sideline net. "I think he's still on the outside of his range," explains Cris Collinsworth, which is a nice way of saying that nobody has a lot of confidence in Matt Bryant and the Giants kicking game. Junkin throws warm-up snaps on the sideline while Collins throws incomplete to Amani Toomer on the field. The Giants are trying desperately to not put the game on their kicker's shoulders.

With six seconds remaining, Bryant and the field-goal team jog onto the field where they are immediately "iced" as San Francisco burns its final timeout. This is the moment where Junkin can atone for his previous bad snap and render it gone forever. A successful kick wins the game and sends New York onto the next round of the playoffs. There are two Niners lined up over Junkin—one on each "half" of his blue helmet. The crowd is in full throat. It is the kind of beautiful and pregnant moment the league and its fans live for.

A replay shows that Junkin double clutches the ball for a split second before throwing his snap low and left, where it is trapped against the grass by his holder, who then tries to scramble and throw up a lame desperation pass. It flutters to the ground. Star Giant defensive end Michael Strahan storms off the field wearing his helmet.[1] The 49ers and their fans mob the playing surface. Somewhere Junkin suffers alone.

"The Giants added Junkin during the week . . . and two poor snaps may have cost them the chance to advance in the playoffs," Buck intones. Today, Junkin is held up as an example of what happens when we try to go to the well one time too many. By coming out of retirement and trying to fly too close to the sun, Junkin crashed. There is a head-shaking, "Well, he should have known better," tone to Junkin-related discussions. There are hushed-tone, "Isn't it a shame" articles written about him year after year.

After the game, and in the days to follow, Junkin sat dutifully at his locker and took blame for the defeat. His teammates generally agreed in their silence on the matter. He didn't hide in the training room, as many before him have done. He did what we would all be proud for our children to do in a similar situation—he accepted his fate like a man.

He then flew home to Louisiana and drank for three days straight.

* * *

The hours following the NFL draft are nervous ones for Jon Akemon. He whiles away the time working out (he sends me video), snapping (he sends video again), bowling (no video), and hanging out with his girlfriend. He has been promised an invite to a postdraft minicamp by an NFL club, the identity of which he won't disclose to me. The coyness betrays an interesting dichotomy of identity for the unsigned snapper. Is Jon Akemon the promising, up-and-coming long snapper about to be signed by and subsequently flown to an NFL club for a weekend consisting of practices, free swag, and the promise of a camp invite? Or is he a guy who drives a forklift at a beer distributorship in Louisville who can't quite let go of the football dream? The answer is, of course, both. But for Jon Akemon, life feels a lot better when it's the former.

Maybe it's my age, but I have an ominous feeling about his situation. There is nothing binding the unnamed club to Jon right now, besides a verbal agreement to bring him in. "My agent is working on the details right now," he tells me via phone while I drive through the mid-South with my kids, in search of a Chick-fil-A but settling, sadly, for KFC. Our lives are vastly different.

I try to strike a fatherly tone with Jon as he waits . . . and strike the balance between encouraging and realistic. "Just be patient and don't make football your entire identity," I tell him. "You definitely have the talent and drive to make it, but there are a lot of variables at play." It's nothing he hasn't heard before.

"People treat you differently when you're signed," he says. What he is describing is the existential dilemma that happens when actually living your dream isn't nearly as cool as just having the dream. He's describing that phenomenon wherein, when you do something cool, people can tend to feel threatened by it and treat you worse as a result. Simply stated, people are comfortable with the "aspiring NFL player Jon Akemon" and less so with the "almost actual NFL player" Jon Akemon because it casts their accomplishments, or lack thereof, in a different light.

Akemon is sweating because there was a snapper drafted (Navy's Joe Cardona, to the Patriots) and there were a handful of others signed to minicamp or tryout deals after the draft. I watch the signings with interest now and imagine the likelihood of a team bringing a certain thirty-nine-year-old writer into a camp for a journalistic exercise-slash-tryout. The idea seems so preposterous that I don't share it with Akemon. I choose, for now, to live my dreams through him.

"To even be in this position is amazing," I say to him, by way of signoff, and by way of encouragement. "You're living my dream."

5

THE RUBIO ZONE

Within the first few moments of my phone call with preeminent snapping instructor Chris Rubio, he has diagnosed my chief snapping problem. "You're too smart," he explains. "Intelligent guys have trouble with this job because you think too much. Thinking a lot serves you well when you write books but not when you snap. The less intelligent guys literally *can't* overthink it—which is wonderful for them!"

He is, of course, right. Just as he was right about quitting his secure post-UCLA gig as a middle-school teacher to start a kicking academy with former Bruin teammate Chris Sailer, back when everybody who had played a down of high-level football anywhere was starting an academy (meaning, usually, just building a website). Just as he was right about giving away lots of free content on his websites and blogs—such as snapper rankings and video segments that have not served to dilute the product and hurt his business but in fact done the opposite. It has made Rubio the most recognized name in an almost completely unrecognized business.

"I got my start here, and I came to all these camps when I was in high school," said current Cleveland Browns long snapper Christian Yount on a Rubio promotional video. "It got me into college and then into the pros, and there's no other camp that's going to give you the same kind of instruction as Rubio Long Snapping." Yount looks very much the pro athlete in this segment, resplendent in a Browns cap with the NFL shield front and center. He is that to which every Rubio camper aspires.

"I want to be the first thing that comes up when you Google 'long snapping,'" Rubio explains. He is currently the second thing that comes up, but I wouldn't bet against him.

In my case he is right about the over-thinking thing because, even as a position player, I would spend an inordinate amount of time thinking about snapping, which I was technically good at but still obsessed over with alarming and miserable regularity. I dreaded special-teams period in practice. And I never had anyone tell me to relax. In fact, my high school coaches made nearly every mistake outlined in a short Rubio video on how to coach and interact with high school long snappers. It wasn't really their fault—back then, nobody was talking about coaching long snappers.

"Don't ever expect them to snap perfectly without warming up," he explains. "You wouldn't throw a quarterback in there ice cold and expect perfection. So why expect it from your snapper? And don't ever say, 'Just go over there by yourself and snap' without showing him any technique or giving any help. You wouldn't say to a linebacker, 'Just go over there and teach yourself how to tackle.'" My coaches, of course, did all of this.

"The main thing is that the kids are having fun," Rubio says of his camp experiences. "You can't snap well if you're nervous. I've never seen a tense kid snap well. And I tell them that they're just throwing a dead animal between their legs, not working for NASA. It's not the end of the world. Nobody is dying if they throw it over the punter's head. I've seen too many kids get too 'into' it. They over-snap."

Of course, getting "too into" something is a fine line, and our society's penchant for obsession is one reason that Rubio has such a successful business model. He is catering to not only obsessive children but also their more obsessive parents. He receives upward of five hundred e-mails and texts a day, most of them from parents. "I'll have a dad of an eighth-grader e-mail me and say, 'Baylor's snapper is a freshman . . . and if he redshirts and then graduates on time my son could potentially have his job,'" Rubio says. "Most of my replies are of the 'relax and have fun' variety."

Rubio's e-mail signature is longer than many online "breaking news" items today, which is a commentary on both Internet news and the way the Internet has shaped long snapping.

CHRIS RUBIO

President and Owner
Rubio Long Snapping
E-Mail: Rubio@RubioLongSnapping.com
Web: RubioLongSnapping.com
Blog: RubiosBlog.com
Twitter: @TheChrisRubio
Facebook: Rubio Long Snapping
YouTube: RubioLongSnapping

I remember as a high school student lining up a sheet of paper in my family's typewriter and typing letters to the various schools to which I was trying to sell my services as a long snapper. They may have requested film, in which case, I would drop a crudely edited (by another high school student) VHS tape in a big, bulky package and drop it in the mail. And then there was the waiting. The result was a few schools offering preferred walk-on status as a position player, with the added bonus of snapping ability.

Today the landscape is much different. Through his website, blog, Twitter, Facebook, and YouTube channels, Rubio has branded himself as the conduit to a college scholarship. Quite simply, Rubio identified a need and filled it before anyone beat him to the punch. Boutique long-snapping instruction had been around before Chris Rubio, but he's the one who brought it to the Internet age, as each day he fills Twitter feeds with tweets about upcoming camps and rankings of high school snappers. Much of it is just subjective noise, but it fills a purpose deeper than actual rankings of fourteen-year-olds, most of which are inconsequential and could be derailed by anything ranging from puberty to a girlfriend breakup. What it is, is a constant barrage of content marketing.

To wit, Rubio announced the signing of California high school snapper Koby Walsh to a preferred walk-on deal at the University of Kentucky. Walsh, an otherwise nondescript-looking six foot zero and 215-pound high school kid, has been to no less than fourteen Rubio-sponsored events since 2012. He is, in that way, the model Rubio student in that he is constantly filmed, ranked, and promoted in the Rubio pipeline. He is also a player who, physically, would never have had a prayer of playing at the Division I level were it not for long snapping. The existence and promotion of a Chris Rubio has made it possible for him.

"Very solid weekend for Koby at VEGAS XXVI in May," Rubio wrote on his site. "Form is great and when he snaps the ball with full power, he is absolutely dominant. Snapping as hard as possible and making sure all of his power is coming back towards the punter will be the keys moving forward and up the rankings. Moves *really well* on his feet with almost surprising athleticism. Tremendous attitude.

The above copy accompanied several photos of Walsh and links to videos of his performances at every Rubio camp. There are several times listed for his snaps, along with an explanation of something called the Rubio Standard Index, which didn't exist a few years ago:

EVENT ELITE—2015
Average 15 yard snap time at VEGAS XXVI: .78
Average 40 yard dash time at VEGAS XXVI: 5.27
RSI VEGAS XXVI: 32.22
(Please note: RSI is the Rubio Standard Index. RSI is the time snap time divided by their score on the Target. Bonus points can be earned for faster snap times. The higher the score, the better the Long Snapper did on the Target.)

It literally chronicles every step of his journey from awkward, gawky early high schooler to battle-tested Division I prospect. The Rubio site is full of such profiles, which make for boring/fascinating reading. His list of 2015 signees—kids who have been to his camps or were otherwise helped to the next level by him—is astonishing in its depth and breadth. It spans nearly every level of college football and every region in the country; here is a sampling:

- Blake Ferguson—LSU
- Riley Lovingood—Tennessee
- Liam McCullough—Ohio St.
- Jake Hale—Ohio
- Ben Makowski—Purdue
- Garrett Wilson—Wake Forest
- AJ Carty—Washington
- Wesley Farnsworth—Nevada
- Tanner Kern—Lafayette College
- Harley Whitehouse—Missouri
- David-Michael Carrell—Southern

- Nick Wildberger—Blinn
- Mike Taylor—Ole Miss
- Tyler Griffiths—NC State
- Nick Cox—Penn St.
- Connor Kubala—Coastal Carolina
- Ryan Farr—Florida
- Harrison Hoffman—Air Force
- Matt Foley—BYU
- Drew McCracken—Kennesaw St.
- Chaska Moon—Virginia Tech
- Grant Merka—Mercer
- Elias McMurry—Appalachian St.
- Carson Vey—University of Pennsylvania
- Joe Gallinghouse—Davidson College
- George Madden—Arkansas
- Tipa Galeai—TCU
- Steven Nixon—Mercer
- Jay Zier—St. Olaf
- Bobby Daggett—Ole Miss
- Zach Sandlin—North Park University
- Hunter Colonna—Gardner Webb
- Sam Walkingstick—Oklahoma St.
- Brandon Storebo—South Dakota
- Michael Pifer—Navy
- Jordan Laube—Bryant
- Harrison Goebel—NAU
- Payton Pardee[1]—Houston

The premise behind content marketing is that if I give you a little bit of product for free—say a short long-snapping instructional video—you'll probably visit my site again and pay me a lot of money later, for one of the more expensive products I offer. Rubio is forever posting short videos of snappers and camps—free content—so that people will pay for his camps and individualized instruction, geared at getting scholarships for kids.

The camp agendas, to me, look joyless and boring. It seems like pressure-packed moments of intensive head-to-head snapping competition interspersed with lots of boring, repetitive work, which is of course what it takes to get good at such a specialized skill. I'm reminded that great athletes can not only block out feelings of anxiety and pressure but also triage and manage all of the boring things they're asked to do. The fact that the *goal* of the Rubio camps is to create a market for players who will do *nothing* but throw a ball between their legs in college for four to five years is astonishing. The fact that he gets people to pay a significant amount of money for this both is and isn't at all surprising.

"My return rate is 99 percent," he explains. "A lot of it is personality and how you speak to the kids and parents." Rubio's approach to coaching is refreshingly simple. He asks players, "Did you have fun and try your hardest? Then it was a good day."

In the age of the Internet marketer, presentation often takes precedence over the actual product, a maxim that rings true in Rubio's case.[2] He never played a down in the NFL but has more clients than guys such as Justin Snow and Bryan Pittman, who have launched boutique snapping schools after their long, successful NFL careers. Granted, they serve different clientele and have different goals. But Rubio is relentless and calculating about his marketing effort. Everything from logo design to the constant tweeting and the uniform quality of the YouTube videos is meant to entice and matter to the next aspiring high school snapper.

Rubio's claim to football fame was a college career at UCLA in which he was on full scholarship for three seasons and never once botched a snap. He walked on at UCLA and was awarded a scholarship two years in. With teammate and kicker Chris Sailer, he parlayed that experience into a special-teams school (Sailer Kicking) and from there built the mini-empire that is Rubio Long Snapping. He was featured in a 1997 *LA Times* interview with Bill Plaschke in which he was portrayed as both a respected cog in the UCLA machine and something of an oddity by teammates, who kept calling him "the fat guy" and urging him to "put a shirt on." The article also said that the specialists were known to "retire to the locker room and watch TV." But Rubio also explained that opponents routinely spit on the football and shout "I'm gonna kill you" before each pressure-packed snap. He remembers his first college snap.

"I was a redshirt freshman and made the trip to Arizona State as a backup," he recalls.

It was about 160 degrees on the field. We were up by like sixty points, and starting in the second quarter the coach kept saying, "Rubio, be ready, you're going to go in." I fired about eight hundred warm-up snaps on the sideline. At halftime I was a mess. I was snapping in the locker room. Finally, in the fourth quarter we lined up to kick a field goal and the coach sent me in. But when I bent down over the ball I couldn't remember where to put the ring finger on my dominant hand. I literally forgot my grip. Everybody was exhausted, and I was bent over the ball, trying to figure out where to put my hands. Finally, a monster defensive tackle from Arizona State, standing right in front of me, said something I'll never forget. He said, "Just snap the ball motherfucker." And I said, out loud, "Okay." And I snapped it, and it was fine. And it was actually a good bit of advice.

Still, as a parade of higher-profile UCLA teammates came and went—guys like Cade McNown, DeShaun Foster, and J. J. Stokes—the current slim version of Rubio may be the only one still making his living in football. "We would come in after games and my teammates would be all beat up, and they'd say, 'Rubio, you're not even sweating.' And I'd be like, 'Yeah, because I played like nine plays today.'"

Mere moments after my first personal e-mail exchange with Rubio, I am receiving his bulk marketing e-mails. The first one features a super-close-up of Rubio's bald pate and sunglasses, staring off into the distance with the requisite "intense" football sneer (with another less close distance-staring sneer shot as the top banner picture). Smiling, in this culture, is highly (pun intended) frowned upon. The message touts the number of 2015 college long-snapping commits so far under the mega-headline "EXPOSURE." Readers are encouraged to "be a part of greatness" and are told "what the Rubio long-snapping family is all about." Like most great brands of our era, the message is more about the culture than the actual instruction (which is also quite good). Being a part of the Rubio long-snapping family (or any long-snapping family—what is this?) is viewed as a good thing.

It's hard to argue with Rubio's results. His first camp had eight participants. His last? Three hundred snappers. I ask him if he gets bored with his job—with basically devoting his life to the practice of, as he says, throwing a ball between his legs. "June and July are my worst months," he explains. "By the end of July I'm burned out on myself! But teaching things to different kids keeps things fresh. They all have different personalities."

"It gives a lot of the, let's say, less athletic kids a chance to get on the field," he says, of snapping. "Some of those kids were my campers, and some of them play in the NFL now. I don't need to market or call college coaches on behalf of players anymore. I'm not the used-car-salesman type. Guys like that end up over-promising, and then looking bad if their guy doesn't pan out. Colleges aren't really listening to high school coaches on a position like this."

Colleges are, in fact, listening to Rubio and then offering scholarships or preferred walk-on opportunities to his players. Over 95 percent of all long-snapping scholarships awarded each year go to Rubio's campers. And he has an agreement to place snappers in the prestigious UnderArmour and U.S. Army All-American games. He blogs daily with rankings on snap speed, target accuracy, forty times, and overall snapping ability. He gives colleges the tools they need to shop online for long snappers and in doing so has created a mini-empire. On his You-Tube page recently, there was snapping tape available on a class of 2020 prospect from Texas, a kid named Cade who not too many years ago was learning to read and tie his shoes. His voice is still high and squeaky, and his snaps are soft, rainbow spirals. Still, he has the hardened, squinty gaze of the college prospect. He is in junior high.

"We have twenty-three locations with Rubio-certified long snappers," he explains. "I'd rather them be taught the way I want them taught. It's all balance, extension, and follow-through. It's all form. When I'm working with a kid it's like sending a huge boat off to sea. I'd rather not have to scrape off moss and barnacles the next time I see him. I don't want to have to fix things that somebody has taught him incorrectly."

Rubio's camps all sell out, despite their significant price tag—$350 for a one-day camp. According to the website, "Every long snapper that attends the camp will get the most exposure possible to college coaches. Each long snapper will be ranked and receive a player profile and YouTube video (included in cost of camp). All results will be blasted throughout the world to reporters and college coaches on social media and by e-mail."

One envisions "reporters"—itself an antiquated word with funny credential-in-fedora connotations—sitting in newsrooms waiting for the rankings from the Chris Rubio Aurora Snapping Camp to come over the wire. But people love language like this, and without even knowing it, Rubio is using the time-tested creative nonfiction trick of taking something relatively ordinary and making it seem epic. "Parents are heavily encouraged to attend *all* aspects of the camp," continues the site. And each camp includes a "recruiting meeting," which ostensibly gives parents and players the ins and outs of an increasingly complicated recruiting process but also, more importantly, implies that there *will* be a recruiting process. This is part of selling the dream, and it is very important.

A few years ago, it was unusual for high school *seniors* to receive scholarship offers solely to snap. Now Rubio is seeing his juniors offered, occasionally, as the industry moves toward greater specialization. "Now people are texting me and freaking out that their junior hasn't been offered," he says, semi-wearily. He recognizes that a significant part of his job involves playing armchair psychologist to youth sports parents.

"I think high school and youth coaches overcoach the game," he explains. "I meet with coaches all the time in my job—college and pro coaches—and sometimes I ask them how many plays they'd run as a youth football coach. More often than not, they say they'd have five plays—and no more. Football is essentially a simple game. We overcomplicate it."

In my opinion, the showpiece video in the Rubio collection is about three minutes of snapping with Yount, by then a Cleveland Brown, in an open suburban field, in longish grass, on a windy day. Yount snaps dozens of balls, all perfect. It is something to aspire to.

Rubio tries to simplify snapping, even in a complicated market. "You get guys trying to be all scientific about it," he says. "Just snap the damn ball. Even though at UCLA we had 105,000 people watching in the Rose Bowl, and maybe another eight million on television . . . the majority of the world couldn't really give a crap about what's happening in the Rose Bowl."

6

BRYAN PITTMAN

The Security Man

Long before becoming an NFL long snapper, Bryan Pittman was a security guard for a freight company. "I marked off fifteen yards and set up a target on the side of a big freight canister," he explains, of the long, solitary days on the job. There, alone, Pittman would perfect his long snapping stroke—a boring, repetitive task that he would repeat for hours and days on end, rain or shine. "If the football made a loud thud I knew I missed," he says. "If it was a soft thud, I knew I was on target."

Pittman's roundabout journey to an NFL paycheck included stops at a community college, the University of Washington, and the semi-pro (nonpay, adult-amateur) Puget Sound Jets. "There were guys that I played with in semi-pro that should have been in the NFL, and guys in the NFL that shouldn't have been there," he says. "At some level you're written off playing semi-pro."

I lived the life of the semi-pro snapper, playing for teams in such forgettable cities as Muncie, Indiana, and Jackson, Michigan, snapping bald, slick practice footballs that felt like beach balls. I quit semi-pro football as a young father, after somebody pulled a gun in a locker-room fight. I had had enough, but I agree with Pittman that the talent on the field, at times, was astonishing, and the football itself was really, really fun.

What was unique about semi-pro was that it was so loosely organized that the games themselves didn't carry any pretense that they "mattered" to anyone. No one tracks or follows the records of semi-pro teams, and for the most part, nobody really comes to the games. I always felt kind of unreasonable even asking my wife to show up, given that she'd be sitting alone in some sad, middle-school bleachers, listening to piped-in hip-hop and hoping that the game wouldn't degenerate into a big fight, as it sometimes did. In semi-pro, "practice" is just an abstract concept, which usually means a dozen (if you're lucky) guys showing up on an even sadder field, in an even sadder part of town, and trying to "get something accomplished" (in coach parlance) in spite of the small numbers.

Semi-pro game nights were an exercise in patiently waiting for teammates to show up, right up until kickoff, as guys drove themselves because the teams couldn't afford buses. Of course, what was great about this is that all of this half-assedness just confirmed in my own fragile mind that none of it mattered. And if none of it mattered, nobody would be disappointed if I screwed up because nobody was watching/caring. Even my teammates on the sidelines spent half the games chatting up girls in the stands or trying to pick up cheerleaders. This was a perfect psychic environment in which to be a snapper because it was the closest thing possible to being alone in my basement. As a result, I snapped wonderfully in semi-pro. I never had a bad snap.

And while the whole thing felt like a self-indulgent waste of time—especially after I became a father—it was truly *fun* in that it was the closest football ever came to feeling like a game to me.

Pittman continues describing his journey to the NFL: "I got interest from Oregon coming out of high school," Pittman explains. "But my grades were bad. I had a partial scholarship to JUCO, and lots of Division II and Division I-AA offers. But my best friend got a full ride to the University of Washington, and I said 'I'm going with him.'" Pittman played for a season with the Huskies, but the promise of a scholarship never came to fruition. "I was a broke college student," he says. "So I stopped going to class and just focused on getting better." Pittman had workouts with the Seattle Seahawks and New England Patriots but wasn't signed.

"That's when I fell back to semi-pro," he says. "I just wanted to get to a camp. I'd go back to the pro days at Washington each spring and work out for scouts because Washington always opened those up to ex-players. But it's like . . . it's not like you're getting mocked . . . but you're kind of looked down upon for going back year after year after not getting signed."

I imagine Pittman driving his own, personal, poor-college-kid car to a lot adjacent to the UW Indoor Training Facility, which like all such facilities is constructed to be as gleaming, impressive, and nonwelcoming as possible. I imagine him walking through the glass and steel double doors, looking big, and perhaps even wearing some dated UW swag left over from his season as a player. I imagine him explaining to the girl at the desk that he's "Bryan Pittman, here for the Pro Day," and then having her ask if he's a player or a scout because she doesn't recognize him and his name may or may not be on the list. I imagine him awkwardly insisting that his name is on the list, before finally being let in, and finding a section of empty FieldTurf on which to stretch. I imagine the delicate male dance of finding someone to catch his warm-up snaps, and the awkward chitchat that would undoubtedly have to be made with players he doesn't know.

Yeah, it sounds horrible. I don't blame him for going back to semi-pro.

✿ ✿ ✿

Speaking of semi-pro, I am strongly considering a return to it as I search for a last, successful snapping experience for this book. Thus far I have queried a team in the Arena Football League (AFL; Philadelphia, via a connection with Jon Akemon), the FXFL (Fall Experimental Football League; via a connection to coach Terry Shea), and a start-up professional indoor league based in the South. I had one positive response from the league—a team called the Pineywoods Bucks who will play their games in what looks like a bull-riding arena near Tyler, Texas (boyhood home of Earl Campbell). On the plus side, they saw my raw snapping film and want to sign me. On the downside, odds are fifty-fifty that they'll fold before the beginning of the season. Still, owner Michael Dixon's enthusiasm is infectious: "Sounds great!" he writes of my idea to snap in a game.

> In a perfect world I would like to make it happen in Texas, at one of my home games. Maybe in our league opener? It may also be cool, if everything goes well, to invite you back to snap in a playoff game. Maybe go with the angle, "The first time it was for the book; this

time it's because we're putting the best twenty-one players on the field to win a playoff game." I'm a promoter, and that means nothing is too crazy to try!

I'm touched, and motivated, by his enthusiasm, and it makes me want to snap perfectly so that I can *earn* my way onto the field, rather than just talking or writing my way on to one.

Mike strikes me as a guy who may be in a little over his head with this endeavor, but I'm continually disarmed by his honesty and encouraged by his faith. Honesty is in short supply in the bravado-first world of football. I try to check in with Mike weekly, to see where he stands in the endeavor—both to encourage him and to make sure that I'll still have a uniform to wear come spring. "I try to serve God in everything that I do," he writes once. He clearly loves football and loves sports entertainment, as he's a former professional wrestler (yikes) and promoter. One of the first times we talk, he shares not only a heartbreaking story about the team's financial straits but also the fact that he had a team pulled out from under him a year ago, when he was in the hospital dealing with serious health issues.

He asks me to pray for him, which I do. "Sorry to be negative," he writes. "Like I said, a little down, but I know it's temporary!"

I admire people who can choose to be positive in all circumstances. In spite of my faith in a God who loves me and ordains my steps, I still at times struggle to do this. As such, I decide to cover my bases and do my due diligence in looking for other teams.

Truth be told, I'm querying teams all the time. There's a semi-addictive quality about wanting to reach out, dream, and then get good news from someone who will agree to put me on a field again. The desire to do this—to search another team's website, find contact information, and send a cold e-mail—seems almost like a sickness, and I realize that I may not ever be satisfied. I don't know if this is normal behavior—meaning, I don't know if other men my age are doing things like this, just in other areas. I know that other men compulsively use pornography, motorcycles, golf, or whatever, which is my justification for continuing to snap against a wall in my house.

I have my head turned, online, by a team with a nice website called the Memphis Blast, which is part of something called the Gridiron Developmental Football League (GDFL), which bills itself as "Memphis Pro Football." Intrigued, I send the e-mail, and before the day is finished—and in fact while I'm on my way to my son's sixth-grade graduation—my phone rings with a Memphis number. I pick up. My dad is in the front seat, and I don't necessarily want to tell him about this yet, as I know there may be some judgment from him as to the wisdom of a thirty-nine-year-old family man suiting up again.

A few seconds into the call, it's clear that I'm on a speakerphone with two gentlemen, one of whom is commissioner of the GDFL and the other who is head coach of the Blast. They talk. A lot. In the parking lot of the school I step out of the car. The boys are confused, and my dad is annoyed that I'm on the phone in his presence, as my parents are slow to accept the cell phone as a routine part of everyday life in the twenty-first century. They talk about the formation of the league, their desire to see it as a developmental platform and a legitimate minor league—all things that have failed miserably in football every single time they've ever been attempted previously.

As they talk, I think of all the reasons I don't want to do this and am reminded of the peculiar but particular sadness I felt as a semi-pro player, driving alone into some sad junior high school parking lot in the ghetto part of a given town; getting my gear out of the trunk; putting it on; and making small talk with guys I didn't know, from walks of life I didn't understand. The thought of that made my bowels clench. But I also remember the peculiar and particular excitement of putting on my gear; pulling on a game jersey (any game jersey); listening to hip-hop bumping through some crummy stadium's crummy sound system; and getting excited because I was about to play *ball*.

"Ted, we'd be honored to have you on the Blast and think you'd bring a lot to the organization," the coach explains. "I really look forward to coaching you." Hmm. We say our good-byes. I finally make my way into a crowded gymnasium, where I watch my child take yet another step toward becoming a man, fully cognizant of the fact that I may have just taken another significant step back toward childhood.

* * *

In my basement snapping I have hit a wall—literally and figuratively. The folding chair I've been propping against the wall and using as a target is coming to pieces. And I seem to have hit a plateau in my improvement. My velocity is good and my accuracy is on point about three-fourths of the time, which isn't nearly good enough. I'll snap five great balls and then, inexplicably, bounce one back, or fire one up high off the basement wall, such that it ricochets throughout the room and bounces off my kids' toys. This usually elicits a reaction from Maxim, who says, "Ooh, bad one, Dad!" My boys have gotten used to my daily sojourns into the basement, and they're used to seeing Dad bent over a football. They have no idea, really, how not normal this behavior is because they have no idea, really, how not controllable most of adult life is. Snapping is an attempt to, as athletes cliché-ishly say all the time, "control what you can control."

Control is eluding me, and I don't know what to do about it.

After my talk with Kevin Gold, he sent me a list of snappers whose stories I should explore for the book. One of the names on the list was Pittman's. I find some Pittman video online—the kind of fluffy, soft-focus segment put together by team websites. In it, Pittman explains (mostly boringly) the nuances of long snapping to a girl in a Texans polo who looks like she just graduated from college and couldn't care less. It's breezy, and they're alone on a practice field. Every team does features like this, and long snappers are good candidates for them, because their jobs are semi-relatable in that they're not using world-class speed to run down a field and they're usually able to be halfway articulate about what it is that they do.

"You want your feet about shoulder width apart and your back flat," says Pittman. "You should be able to put a two-by-four on your back. Then you want your arms straight and a smooth, steady motion. No hitches and no pickups." He then fires the ball back to the college girl. Giggling ensues as she drops the first couple.

One thing about the segment stands out to me, and it's a tiny detail: Pittman's placement of the index finger on his right (snapping) hand. As he explains it, he slides the index finger up so that it is parallel to the seam of the ball, rather than just letting it wrap around the ball as is usually the norm. "I do this to keep the ball from going high," he explains.

This is a lightbulb moment.

I pause the video and head to the basement, quickly, before hustling the boys off to school. I bend over the ball and exhale, trying Pittman's grip. The result is, for a snapper, semi-miraculous. I fire the first fifteen-yard punt snap back and knock my pylon target off the top of the chair. I bend over another ball, just to make sure it wasn't a fluke. Same thing. A laser. I reconfigure the target for field-goal snaps and take the same grip. Same result: the satisfying thwack of ball hitting target. I smile and bound up the stairs, ashamed that it has taken something so small and insignificant to give me hope.

⋄ ⋄ ⋄

Bryan Pittman sent a cold e-mail of his own once, to emerging agent Kevin Gold. At that point, he was just another guy with a year of college experience, who hadn't been signed after three UW pro days. "I told him I had film, and had been playing, and he suggested I go to a camp in Reno for specialists," Pittman recalls. "These were all special-teams coaches who knew what to look for in specialists. Sometimes even scouts don't really know what to look for. Remember [former Dallas Cowboys legend] Bill Bates? He lined up against me and gave me rushes."

As a result of the camp, Pittman was flown into Cleveland for a private workout—the kind where the athlete is flown in, shuttled from the airport, and then just dresses and snaps. It must be an excruciating kind of pressure, to know that your vocational future rests on such an audition. At the Browns facility, nestled in a residential neighborhood in Berea, Ohio, Pittman snapped for coaches and scouts. And the Browns signed him and invited him to camp. Unfortunately, it was the year they drafted Ryan Pontbriand in the fifth round—the highest selection of a pure snapper in league history—and Pittman was summarily released.

But Pontbriand held out, giving Pittman a taste of his first NFL camp. "I got a job painting houses," he recalls. "I was up on a ladder, and the coach called and said, 'Wanna come play?' Their guy was holding out. Eventually he signed and they released me, but two days later I was signed by the Houston Texans."

Pittman recalls an atmosphere of acceptance in the locker room because, at the time, the franchise was only two years old, and he was a relatively aged twenty-six. Walking into a locker room as a twenty-six-year-old man is a far different thing than walking in as a raw rookie, fresh off the college campus.

"I also played on the scout team," he recalls. "That was one reason [head coach Gary] Kubiak and I didn't get along. He wanted me to play tight end, and I just wanted to snap. I knew I wasn't going to be Jeremy Shockey, running around catching touchdown passes." Pittman knew that his future in the league was in snapping the football, and a mashed pinkie or dislocated shoulder as a result of playing tight end could have seriously derailed that future.

He recalls an especially brutal subzero Sunday afternoon in Chicago's Soldier Field as the worst snapping conditions he faced. "My mouthpiece was frozen into my facemask," he says. But he still snapped perfectly. And it wasn't a frozen field in Chicago that ended his streak of five hundred perfect snaps. It was the dreaded *Sports Illustrated* jinx.

The scene at Qualcomm Stadium was surreal to begin with, as thousands of Southern Californians had been displaced to the stadium by wildfires, and the team was forced to train off-site.

"I was written up in *SI* because I had a streak of four or five hundred perfect snaps or something," he says.

> We were playing in San Diego, and they always poured a ton of paint on the midfield logo on those fields. Anyway, I knew it didn't feel right . . . the way my cleats caught in the paint, and as a result, my butt went up in the air and the ball flew about ten yards over the punter's head. San Diego's cornerback [Antonio] Cromartie picked up the ball and just jogged into the end zone. It was the easiest touchdown he'd ever scored.

"It was hard to go back out and do it after that," he says. "But the next one was fine."

I ask Pittman how he dealt with the constant nerves of the job. "If you're not nervous, something is wrong with you," he says of the occupational hazard. Pittman points out that he was never released from a contract as a pro, but it was a strange suspension that unraveled the snapper's confidence and led to the end of his career. In 2008, Pittman was suspended for using a weight-loss diuretic that is often used as a masking agent for anabolic steroids. Pittman had struggled in 2008 and was beginning to face criticism from local media.

"Anyone who has watched the Texans this year knows they've had trouble with the long snaps," wrote a columnist from the *Houston Press*. "One snap possibly cost the Texans three points on Monday night when

Pittman had trouble getting the ball back to holder Matt Turk. I don't know what that has to do with steroids, but the NFL might have done the Texans a big favor here." After the gaffe he was named, again in *Sports Illustrated*, as columnist Peter King's "Goat of the Week."

Pittman missed the final four games of the 2008 season, and after a handful of games in Atlanta (and three back in Houston) in 2009, he was done. Today he's an insurance agent, high school football coach, and father in the Houston suburbs.

"It killed my confidence level," he says, of the controversy surrounding the suspension. This speaks to the fragile mental and emotional state of the snapper, whose mind must be relatively unburdened in order to perform the task at hand. "I couldn't snap the way I used to." Pittman had a workout with the Ravens in 2010 and, for a few years after, would still receive calls from teams.

"The last call came in 2012," he says. "The first few years were rough. It's hard to sit there and be on standby."

7

TREVER KRUZEL

The Minicamp Body

The last time I was at the Detroit Lions' team facility in Allen Park, Michigan, it was to interview newly minted rookie "franchise" quarterback Joey Harrington for *ESPN the Magazine*. Harrington had just completed a sterling college career at Oregon that culminated in a Heisman campaign that included gigantic photo banners of Harrington on a Manhattan skyscraper. Heady stuff.

Harrington's transition from the geographic grandeur of the Pacific Northwest to the, well, grit of metro Detroit was a difficult one. Allen Park is situated off a highway system that, on its best day, is a little grim. Chunks of the pavement have been blasted out by the relentless freezing and thawing of the Michigan winter, and to be frank, there's just not a whole lot about the Detroit outskirts that is very nice to look at. There is, however, an IKEA.

None of this seemed to have fazed Harrington in the least, when we met, and I left the interview convinced that this young man's combination of talent, looks, and charisma would win over the loyal-but-understandably cynical Detroit fan base and put him on top of the NFL for a long time. Of course, none of that happened.

Harrington's arrival coincided with the opening of Ford Field, the crown jewel in a downtown gentrification plan that never quite "took." The closest the Lions have come to the Super Bowl, ever, has been hosting it at Ford Field (Steelers versus Seahawks) and a long time ago at the old Pontiac Silverdome (49ers/Bengals)—which now stands as a symbol of suburban decay. Harrington, like lots of Lions before and after him, was considered a "bust," though it's always unclear as to whether that's completely the fault of the athlete or more a function of a dysfunctional mess of an organization. It seemed, for a time, like the NFL's Bermuda Triangle—a place where careers went to die.

Still, the Lions have one of the most loyal fan bases in all of pro sports. Losing season after losing season, the stadium continues to fill, jerseys are sold, and fans are eternally hopeful. It's still the dream of most Michigan kids to suit up in Honolulu blue. Former Northern Michigan long snapper Trever Kruzel was no different.

"The drive down was definitely the worst part," says Kruzel, regarding nerves. "I had eight hours just to think about what if this or that goes wrong."

Kruzel works for Fox Motors, selling cars in northern Michigan. He moonlights as a prospective NFL long snapper. He explains that if he's not fully focused on selling cars, he won't make his quotas and won't make a living. Still, he dreams of the NFL and works toward that goal as well.

I imagine him clocking in at the dealership, collecting glossy car brochures, and manning one of those very transient-looking, Formica-topped sad desks that car salesmen inhabit. I imagine him folding his large frame into the passenger's seat for test drives and making polite but totally banal chit-chat with the man or woman next to him who may or may not be purchasing the vehicle. I imagine him extolling the virtues of whatever midsize luxury sedan he's representing. I imagine new-car smell. I imagine him not bringing up his brief tenure with the Detroit Lions because doing so would be show-offy and borderline manipulative in a sales context, and he seems like the kind of guy who wouldn't go for that sort of thing.

I imagine that it must be hard to think about selling cars when one has been so close to the Dream: when there has been an NFL locker, for however short a time, with your stuff in it; and when there have been breathless local-kid-makes-good newspaper stories written about it. It would be hard to pour yourself a Styrofoam cup of break-room coffee and set about the work of selling cars after that.

"It's like I have two completely different careers that need my full attention," he says. "I don't like doing anything halfway. I want to do everything I can for Fox Motors. They've been great to me. I need to not think about football when I'm at work, and not think about work when I'm doing football stuff. I definitely took a different road, being from a DII school, I didn't have a bunch of looks. I knew long snapping would be my ticket."

Unlike some prospects, who snap hundreds of balls every day, Kruzel appears to have some balance in his life. "Between lifting, running, and a Wednesday-night Bible study, I'm usually snapping every other day," he explains. There are differences of opinion on this. There are guys who obsessively snap every day and other guys for whom the less-is-more mantra applies: do enough to maintain the muscle memory, do enough to stay sharp, but don't overdo it.

Players like Kruzel are becoming something of a rarity in modern college football—the nonspecialist specialist. He stood out and made significant contributions as both a defensive end and fullback while at Northern Michigan—alma mater of Steve Mariucci and member of the Great Lakes Intercollegiate Athletic Conference (GLIAC).

The GLIAC plays great football and actually has a rich and interesting history of putting players into the NFL and then seeing those players contribute. Tiny Hillsdale College in Michigan is perhaps best known for championing political conservatism but has also put standout tackle Jared Veldheer (Cardinals) and wide receiver Andre Holmes (Raiders) into the NFL in recent years. Saginaw Valley State tackle Todd Herremans started 124 games for the Philadelphia Eagles, and Wayne State running back Joique Bell was a key contributor (and much-needed feel-good story) for his hometown Detroit Lions in recent years. Tiffin running back Chris Ivory was a standout with the New York Jets and is seeking a significant free agency payday, as "feature" backs are, for the moment, back in demand.

Perhaps the most decorated GLIAC program in the past two decades has been Grand Valley State, which has been a coaching pipeline for such industry stars as Brian Kelly and Brady Hoke, as well as NFL standouts including linebacker Dan Skuta (49ers) and wide receiver Charles Johnson (Vikings) in addition to NFL alumni Jeff Chadwick and Robb Rubick.

"Long snapping was just something I did to help the team out," Kruzel explains. He skipped the Rubio camp circuit and never had formal long-snapping training until visiting Michael Husted's kicking camp before the NFL draft.

In 2014, Kruzel was named Northern Michigan's defensive MVP and honorable mention All-GLIAC, as he started and played in all eleven games on the defensive line. He led the Wildcats in sacks with 5.5 and was fourth on the team with fifty-eight total tackles (thirty-nine solo, nineteen assists). He also had ninety receiving yards on nine catches. The Wildcat football program is unique, in part, because it competes in a wooden dome—known affectionately and informally as the Yooper Dome (actual name: the Superior Dome). The unique wooden structure seats around eight thousand for football.

Michigan's Upper Peninsula is its own, unique culture. Much like a Scandinavian country, summer days are long and radiant, as the sun glints off such postcard-worthy landmarks as the Pictured Rocks National Lakeshore and Tahquamenon Falls. Winter, however, is a seven-months-long siege marked by record snowfalls and the emotional savagery of a latitude so far north that there are only a few precious hours of daylight. The kind of people who survive in the Upper Peninsula are the archetypal tough midwesterners: the kinds of people who own snowmobiles and change their own oil and, when asked how they are, always say "good"; the kind of people who don't see the point in complaining about things; and the kind of people who start sentences with the word "Yeah" and also end sentences with the same word. I admire these strong northerners but still can't shake the feeling that agreeing to go to Northern Michigan would have been, for me, akin to an emotional death sentence.

Kruzel's college tape shows an athletic and active "down" defensive end. The fact that he played every down as a starter and also snapped puts his snapping accomplishments into greater focus—given that the snaps were often performed with banged-up hands and sore shoulders. This is the reason that most programs tab a specialist to snap, making multiuse players like Kruzel a dying breed. His college snapping film is impressive, and his snaps are fast and accurate, often in spite of less-than-ideal Great Lakes–area weather.

"I started focusing on snapping after college," says the six-foot-one, 250-pound Kruzel. He was encouraged by his agent, John Perez of Perez Sports Associates, to attend the Husted Camp. Kruzel flew out to Husted's California camp with his older brother—also a former Northern Michigan long snapper. "My brother and I went to high school together," he explains. "He played Division III baseball as a pitcher and catcher, and just didn't love it. He ended up at Northern Michigan playing football and snapped for two seasons. I came in after he graduated and took over long snapping. You didn't see our team playing on ESPN, so any exposure we were going to get came from camps and pro days.

"It [Husted Camp] was awesome because I'd never done anything like that," he says. "Snapping was always just something I did on the side. Husted's long-snapping guy was a former NFL player named Mitch Palmer. He was really cool in that he didn't try to change anything for the first few sessions. He just watched us snap. But afterward he would just suggest little tweaks."

Kruzel was like a sponge, snapping all morning and often returning on his own in the afternoon to snap some more. "Most guys came from bigger colleges," he says. "And I was struck by how many guys had been doing it for a long time out of college."

Part of the Husted experience included exposure to pro scouts and a videotaped profile. His Husted Camp tape shows a big, thick athlete with pro-ready velocity on punt snaps, and promise on kick snaps as well, despite a little inconsistency. Kruzel's big break, however, came by way of an invite to the Saginaw Valley State University pro day. Even smaller schools will host these predraft auditions as a means of generating interest in their players. Kruzel's agent made a major push to get him in front of pro scouts at the Saginaw Valley pro day.

"That was my first exposure to somebody from the Lions," he says. "He put me through a one-on-one workout and did some snapping stuff. Afterward he talked to me for a long time, just to learn more about me, my family, and my friends."

And then Kruzel . . . went back to selling cars: Formica desk, breakroom coffee, and checking the phone for voicemails and texts. And for many days, the phone didn't ring. "The Packers called once before the draft just to make sure they had the right number for me, but I never heard from them again!" he says.

But on the Saturday morning of his birthday, while at a morning workout with his brother, Kruzel's phone finally rang. "I had just dropped my cleats on the field to change shoes," he recalls. "And the phone rang. It was my agent saying that he talked to the Lions and they were gonna bring me down for their rookie camp." Kruzel went out for a birthday dinner with his family, and the earlier call was confirmed by a formal invitation from Lions assistant director of pro personnel Rob Lohman. "It was one of the coolest calls I've ever gotten."

It was the call that led to the fateful eight-hour car ride, which provided lots of time to think about the opportunity ahead of him. Kruzel knew the Lions had a regular snapper, Don Muhlbach, who had been with the club since 2004. But he also knew he'd be taking every rep in minicamp. When he arrived at the club's Allen Park facility, there was a locker with his name on a nameplate, and a Honolulu-blue jersey, number 50, hanging in his locker. "It was crazy," he says of the experience. "There's no other word to describe it. To be where Calvin Johnson and Matthew Stafford lift and do their thing every day. It didn't seem like it was actually happening to me."

Don Muhlbach's picture would appear next to the terms "incumbent" and "consistent" in the dictionary. A native Texan, Muhlbach snapped for Texas A&M in 2003, after working as a punter in previous seasons. His body of work at A&M was significant enough to land him on the Baltimore Ravens briefly in 2004, before he ended up in Detroit, where he was signed to replace the injured Jody Littleton. Ill-fated former Lions general manager Matt Millen once referred to Muhlbach as "the Nolan Ryan of long snappers." At the end of the 2015 season, Muhlbach was still Detroit's snapper. Muhlbach has survived the tenures of Steve Mariucci, Dick Jauron, Rod Marinelli, Jim Schwartz, and Jim Caldwell. The Lions have, purportedly, "Restored the Roar" countless times during his tenure. Muhlbach has lost 114 games since joining one of the most unsuccessful franchises in the modern history of the NFL.

Kruzel took every punt and kick snap in the minicamp, without incident. "I don't do too bad in high pressure situations," he says. "Once I get the ball in my hands there's no problem." Still, it was the most pressurized situation he'd ever experienced.

"It was crazy to bend down over the football and have every eye in the Lions organization on me," he says. "There was Jim Caldwell standing with his arms folded, taking everything in. All the scouts were on the sidelines, and then multiple 'eyes in the sky' taping everything. Several times I thought, 'Holy crap this could go really bad.' But it went really good. You snap the ball, run down the field, and then jog back and do it again. It's all the same stuff."

Near the end of camp, however, Kruzel was pulled aside by special-teams coach Joe Marciano. Marciano, sixty-one, has the grizzled look and hyper-aggressive vernacular of the longtime NFL special-teams coach and said in his introductory comments that the Lions would "kick off and kick ass." Marciano began his NFL coaching career in 1986 as a special-teams/tight-ends coach for the New Orleans Saints—long before Kruzel was born. Most recently he spent twelve seasons as the special-teams coordinator for the Houston Texans.

The end of minicamp is sort of like the end of summer camp for regular people, in that the week was probably transformative and life changing but then there is the reality of leaving camp and going back to normal, civilian life. For Kruzel, it involved facing the fact that after three magical days, he would no longer be a Detroit Lion.

"He pulled me aside during practice on Sunday and said 'We're not gonna mess with a good thing. But if we get in a bind . . . stay by your phone.'"

8

NOLAN OWEN

The Would-Be Rubio

I say hello to former Northern Illinois Huskie and current boutique snapping coach Nolan Owen and then, an hour later, have heard much of his life story. To say that he's gregarious would be a massive understatement.

He recalls a time when, as an undersized and awkward high school sophomore, current king of the snapping coaches, Chris Rubio, almost told him to hit the road. "He likes to tell the story that I was one more bad snap away from him telling me to find another position," Owen recalls. "Then I snapped again and he saw something in me."

Owen, whose two last names take some getting used to, caught the long-snapping bug on a trip to Dallas Cowboys training camp in Oxnard, California. There, his father pointed out a long snapper warming up on the sideline. "My dad said, 'That's the easiest way for a smaller guy to make a college or NFL roster.' I desperately wanted to play college football . . . so I started snapping. Every day. My first few snaps were laughable. I'd snap into a soccer net, and I'd fire the ball ten feet over the net."

Owen's chief gift, at least initially, seemed to be a preternatural ability to do the same thing, over and over, and not get bored. "I snapped every day," he says. "Hundreds of snaps, every single day. It didn't matter if it was Christmas or my birthday. It didn't matter if I had anybody to catch. I set up targets in the backyard, in parking lots. . . . I snapped every day."

Still, learning a skill like snapping, in a vacuum, proved difficult. "I just thought, 'I'm awful,'" he recalls. But Owen was resourceful. "My sister's boyfriend at the time was an All-American punter at USC [University of Southern California], and my dream was to play at USC. He gave me Chris Rubio's card. Rubio saw me snap and said I was one of the worst long snappers he'd ever seen. But at four weeks he saw progress."

I've long been of a mind that football has to fill a deep emotional need in order for a person to really pursue it. It's too hard otherwise. There's too much potential for physical suffering as well as potential for public shame and ridicule. It's just too hard. Owen's narrative seems to support this theory. If Owen had just snapped thousands of balls each day into a soccer net, and *hadn't* made it, it would be tempting to see his story as sad and tragic—just another lame kid with an unrealistic dream who needed to be gently redirected toward something more "realistic"—except that it worked out.

Owen eventually became a long snapper and a starter at right offensive tackle for one of the biggest and most successful high school football programs in the country. He climbed the Rubio long-snapper rankings and peaked as the number six long snapper in the nation in the class of 2007. "I told my high school coach that I wanted to be a USC Trojan and he laughed at me," Owen recalls. "But by my senior year I was the only one getting letters. I was getting recruited by Oklahoma State, Stanford, Cal, Fresno State, Arizona State, and many other programs."

But then the unthinkable happened. In the fourth game of his senior season he tore the anterior cruciate ligament (ACL) and meniscus cartilage in his knee. He saw the promise of scholarships or preferred walk-on opportunities dwindle, both with the injury and coaching changes at major programs like Stanford and Oklahoma State. Owen saw the injury as a test from God. He could curse his bad luck, or he could immediately get back to work. He chose the latter.

"I went to physical therapy three times a week, for four hours a day," he says. "Four months after surgery I was *fully* cleared by the doctors. I was able to do anything. Full go."

Still unresolved was Owen's status with his beloved USC Trojans, for whom he was pulling out all the proverbial stops. "Every time I visited campus I wore lifts in my shoes," he says. "To try to appear a little taller than I am."

I cringe a little bit at the story but can totally relate. Though the body-image craze is often attributed to young women, male athletes can be every bit as obsessive about their physiques. I remember picking outfits on recruiting visits simply because they showed off the muscle tone I had been so obsessed with in the weight room. I remember weighing myself several times each day, making sure my body weight and muscle mass were climbing to reach major-college or NFL levels. It's sick and weird, but almost every football player I knew operated like this—at least those of us who had to work hard just to hang around.

Owen's USC star appeared to be on the rise when he was invited to campus to work out for some coaches. Little did he know that would include icons Pete Carroll (now a Super Bowl champion with the Seattle Seahawks), Ed Orgeron (iconic for his intensity and recruiting skill), and former USC head coach Steve Sarkisian.

In 2007, the USC Trojan football program was arguably the most glamorous football operation in the country, at any level. The team had just seen the departure of megastars in Reggie Bush and Matt Leinart, who were replaced by the similarly dazzling Mark Sanchez and Joe McKnight. The defensive roster read like a future Pro Bowl squad, featuring names such as Brian Cushing, Rey Maualuga, Keith Rivers, Sedrick Ellis, and Taylor Mays. They were a fixture on the ABC Saturday-night prime-time game. High-profile fans included Will Ferrell and Snoop Dogg. USC was such a practical and cultural juggernaut in Southern California that it even indirectly resulted in the ouster of the NFL's two failed Los Angeles franchises—the Raiders and the Rams—both of whom played in half-empty stadiums in front of indifferent crowds. So-Cali fans only had eyes for one pro football team, and it was the University of Southern California.

To be a USC football player in the mid-2000s was to consider the world your own personal oyster. And the head coach was cool. Pete Carroll seemed to defy every long-standing college head-coach stereotype in that he wasn't the typical bald, florid, joyless dictator. He actually seemed to be enjoying his work, and players seemed to actually enjoy him.

"They said, 'We love you, we know all about the injury, and we still want you to come to USC as a preferred walk-on,'" Owen recalls. It appeared as though all of his USC dreams were coming true, until he received a call from Chris Rubio.

"'I have a full-ride scholarship to Northern Illinois University (NIU), where you'll start as a freshman and play your first game against the University of Iowa in Soldier Field,' Rubio said. They knew that I was committed to USC, but they had a problem at the position and needed somebody right away," Owen recalls. He was on the next plane to De Kalb, Illinois, which is a long way from Los Angeles, both geographically and culturally. Still, the proverbial red carpet was rolled out for the diminutive snapper who, three years prior, would have been a laughable long shot to play college football anywhere.

The Mid-American Conference (MAC) is about as far away culturally from the Pac-12 as one can imagine. Instead of a hipster enclave such as Eugene, Oregon, or cultural/geographic destinations like Palo Alto and Los Angeles, California, the MAC inhabits cities such as De Kalb, Illinois; Toledo, Ohio; and Muncie, Indiana. MAC cities are all the same in that they are a little bit grim, industrial, and sad, with the university providing the little glimmer of hope. My favorite MAC city is Mt. Pleasant, Michigan—home of the Central Michigan Chippewas—which offers nothing in the way of a "mount" or "mountain" and is pleasant only in that it seems like a strip mall that goes for several miles, bookended on one end by a highway and on the other by a large, garish casino.

"They showed me all over the campus, and the current Huskies took me into Chicago to show me the city," he recalls. "I felt really comfortable. I wanted to play right away since I'd missed half of my senior year, and I knew I wouldn't have to pay a cent." Still, there was one last bit of unfinished business. Per National Collegiate Athletic Association (NCAA) rules, Owen wasn't allowed to snap in front of coaches on his official visit. But there was no stipulation against him "happening" to be at the facility at the same time as NIU's punter, happening to put on workout clothes, and then happening to snap some balls. After the session, Owen was ushered into the office of head coach Joe Novak. Novak—thick, bald, ruddy, and intense—was right out of college-football-coach central casting. He played collegiately for legendary hard-ass Bo Schembechler.

The head coach's office is an intentionally intimidating place for teenage boys to be. The coach is generally positioned behind a giant mahogany desk and surrounded by a career's worth of photos, trophies, and memorabilia meant to remind the athlete where he currently sits in the pecking order of the sport. "We're offering a full-ride scholarship, and you'll start for four years," said Novak. "We need to know right away." Owen, who was in town without his parents, said he needed some time to think it over. "You've got forty-eight hours," the coach replied.

A month after signing, Owen was on campus, working out with the team and falling in love with the woman who would become his wife. "She was literally the first woman I met in Illinois," he recalls. "She was a dancer with the NIU dance team, so she was on the field during my games. It was a lot of fun." Owen started every game as a collegian— fifty-two in a row—and snapped 475 total snaps (punt and placekick) without an errant snap. He played against Tennessee, Minnesota, Iowa, Wisconsin, and Fresno State during his career as a Huskie.

"In my junior year of college, four days before the eighth game of the season, my son was born," Owen recalls. It presented a considerable challenge for a full-time student-athlete and his dance-team girlfriend. "We chose life," he says. "We wanted to keep and raise the baby, but it was a huge challenge." Owen had snapped the entire season with a broken collarbone. One of the realities of college football is that if you, say, decide to fix your broken collarbone (the sane response in this situation) you may be replaced, never to be seen or heard from again. Owen instead took pain-killing injections and played the whole season with the fracture, a full schedule of classes, and a newborn baby waking up in the middle of the night for feedings. He was given a couple of days off for the birth of his son but with the understanding that he would be back at practice and snapping later in the week. Big time (or even medium-time) college football waits for nothing—even new life.

Owen says the kinds of demands the program placed on him prepared him for what he thought would be a pro career. "I was rushed on every rep in practice, by the team's best athlete," he says. "Such that when I got into the game I could always snap and block against whoever they put in front of me."

Still, the young family overcame the struggles and learned to raise their son, and Owen was eyeing a potential pro career as he approached graduation. Again, he would face a significant challenge. While covering a punt and trying to dodge the opposition's most athletic linebacker, he planted his foot in the ground. "It wasn't the most athletic play," he says with a laugh. "When I put my foot in the ground I sheared off a quarter-sized piece of my tibia. I took cortisone shots and played the rest of the season, but by the end of our bowl game I could barely walk. I had surgery after the season and that was basically the end of my football career."

❈ ❈ ❈

If this is an especially hard or emotional reality for Owen, he won't let on as he is too busy being enthusiastic about his growing coaching business. I remark that he has a lot of pluck to think that he can wrest a market share from Rubio, his former mentor. [1]

Owen has been full time for six months but has been coaching long snapping and building his clientele for over four years. In many ways, he's doing the same things Rubio is doing—marketing relentlessly, ranking snappers, getting snappers on tape, and coaching a "for granted" aspect of the game with a ton of enthusiasm. Owen builds confidence in his snappers so that they can perform in games and does so by providing them "competitive" snapping situations in his facility. He uses loud music, fatigue, videotape, and pressurized competition to simulate a gamelike experience. The result is a prepared snapper.

The video on Owen's website is revelatory. Each clip shows an impeccably coached snapper, with perfect form, snapping the ball into a tiny target, except that for each rep the other snappers are creating noise and distraction in the background—whacking the turf with giant foam rollers and yelling. Sometimes the music is loud. On one clip, another snapper lays on his back right next to the football and stares up at the snapper, weirdly. There is the distinct impression that while they are men (sort of) preparing for a job (sort of), they are also kids having fun.

"My snappers tell me that snapping in a game is easier than snapping here," he says. "I tell them to remember how many times they've already done it successfully."

9

PERFECT LACES

NFL Coach Gary Zauner

It occurred to me recently that since taking on this project at the beginning of winter, I have been strictly a basement snapper, even though it's now late June. I have my seven-yard and fifteen-yard increments marked on my basement floor—a basement where there is no wind, no precipitation, and consistent footing every time. I decided it was time to venture outside to snap, with the specter of an Fall Experimental Football League (FXFL) or, at the very least, semi-pro experience in Memphis looming large.

I packed up my youngest son, Maxim, and drove him to Michigan State University (MSU), where there is a retro AstroTurf football field inside the MSU track complex. It is open to the public, and I go there often to run routes for a former college quarterback who, like me, can't give it up. The field sits in the shadow of Spartan Stadium—MSU's ever-expanding shrine to the revenue-generating power of big-time college football—and adjacent to its now-requisite-for-every-program indoor practice complex.

I have a love/hate relationship with the old turf in that while it is concrete-like and manifestly awful to play on, I am now nostalgic for it in the way that many older men get nostalgic for almost anything that reminds them of a bygone era. "This is called 'Golden Age thinking,'" explained the douche villain character in Woody Allen's film *Midnight in Paris*. He goes on to explain that Golden Age thinking is the territory of romantics who can't stomach life in the present day.

I like the feel of the Day-Glo green turf underneath my sneakers, and Maxim loves the neatly lined field. He is soon off zigzagging across the turf, playing out a football fantasy of his own creation. This, I think, is what I miss most. He is, in his mind, a beautiful, elegant, confident NFL player, without any of the attendant stress, anxiety, physical pain, and paranoia that actually accompanies that career in real life. I love watching him do this.

I spit on my fingers and then grab the ball and fire a few field-goal snaps into a soccer goal. It's weird snapping targetless, as the net is just sort of big and amorphous and one must imagine where the ball would actually hit a holder's hands. My field-goal snaps are fast, tight, and flawless. I bend over the ball and fire them, almost without thinking about it, which is the goal.

I walk to the fifteen-yard line and place the ball for my punt snaps. This is where it gets interesting. In the basement, I've been drilling my little pylon target pretty consistently—and if not drilling it, then getting in the general neighborhood. Out here, my snaps are consistently low. The problem is that I'm having a little trouble unsticking my shoes from the sticky turf enough to generate good backward thrust. In the basement, I naturally slide backward a little with each punt snap. Out here, it's as though my feet are anchored. I suddenly feel awkward and un-confident, and while I occasionally fire a perfect snap into the middle of the net, I also miss low—a lot. This is not "bounce off the turf" low but more like "skim the punter's shoe tops" low.

Frustrated, I jog to the sideline and run some "gassers," across the field and back. Soon I'm exhausted and dripping sweat. I bend over the ball for a final punt snap. It's low. Dejected, I grab the ball and fire a few more perfect field-goal snaps into the net. At least I have that, for now.

◦ ◦ ◦

Longtime NFL special-teams coach Gary Zauner has built a collection of websites that can only be described as comprehensive and labyrin-thine. He operates CoachZauner.com, CoachZaunersLocker-Room.com, PerfectLaces.com, CoachZaunerKickingCamps.com, CollegeKickingCoach.com, SnappingCoach.com, and the enticingly named PathToProFootball.com. Every site is laden with graphics, images, and links to the other sites. They are all sort of confusingly similar, yet there is the distinct sense that by not looking at all of them, I'm missing something. He has a blog, a Facebook page, a YouTube site, and a Twitter feed.

I'm intrigued by Zauner because I read about his approach in John Feinstein's great book *Next Man Up*, about a season Feinstein spent embedded with the Ravens' staff, of which Zauner was a part. I'm more intrigued because after a career as a small-college kicker and punter, Zauner played semi-pro football in the same league that my father played in, and at the same time: Zauner for the West Allis (WI) Spartans and Dad for the Madison Mustangs.

I click . . . and click. There is Zauner talking about how he worked with Mick Tinglehoff and Paul Krause at a tryout with the Minnesota Vikings. Tinglehoff taught him the tenets of snapping "perfect laces," which are, simply stated, to grab the ball by the laces (like throwing a pass), place the ball on the line, and snap the ball the same way and to the same distance each time so that the ball rotates the same way and the holder gets the laces. It is, conceptually, very simple.

The video packaging is slick and features Zauner in a "Coach Zauner"–branded polo shirt and cap, done in Vikings/Ravens purple and gold. There is video of Zauner working with a Canadian snapper named Jorgen Hus, who attended Zauner's free-agent camp and ended up signing with the St. Louis Rams. Zauner is very exacting in how he describes snapper alignment, going so far as to stipulate where the nose of the ball should be (on the line) and making sure the holder is positioned correctly, right down to the last three-quarters of a yard. He explains how, by rotating the ball one-third of the way left or right, a snapper can snap "perfect laces." It's the most scientific presentation of snapping I've seen thus far and is a corollary to Chris Rubio's "just have fun and snap the damn ball" approach. I tend to be less scientific and more like Rubio in my own approach.

The next video, with free-agent snapper Taylor Jordan, is perhaps the most helpful because, in it, Zauner shows and explains some of Jordan's bad snaps (which, in his defense, aren't that bad at all). This is incredibly freeing because it shows that even good snappers occasionally have trouble, and in addition to the amorphous and troubling "mental issues" diagnosis, there is usually some sort of biomechanical explanation as well. For example, Jordan skips field-goal snaps off the turf because he is dragging the ball and his center of gravity is too low, due to a too-wide stance.

Zauner writes on the site,

> Any kicker and punter will credit success to their snappers. It's a bond that specialists have because of their operation. You may even say it's similar to a quarterback's timing with a receiver running routes. Kickers and punters rely heavily on comfort and concentration, and an errant or wobbly snap can throw everything off balance. A bad snap can even throw a holder off his spot by just a few inches causing a kick to sail wide. I can't say it enough; the snapper is the most vital man in the kicking game!
>
> When I was a punter and kicker in high school and college, I always appreciated having a good snapper because it made my job so much easier. I was only as good as my snapper was. That's why over my high school, college and NFL coaching career, I've always put finding a good snapper at the top of my recruiting and scouting lists.
>
> As a side note, when I was an NFL Special Teams Coach with the Baltimore Ravens, I petitioned for snappers to be a part of both the NFL Combine and the Pro Bowl because I felt that they are a "football player" just as anyone else on the team. With the support and endorsement of several NFL Coaches and Coordinators, the petition was brought to the NFL Competition Committee and passed. Initially, the NFL Combine invited two snappers each year but has since dropped to one. As far as each team having a long snapper for the Pro Bowl, it was decided each team would have a "need" player the coaches select and it's generally understood it's always a snapper.

I don't know if it's Zauner's marketing orientation or just an overall good nature that makes him so quick to return my call, but he is. It's a reminder of how refreshing it is to work with someone outside the confines of the NFL public relations system, where teams treat a ten-minute conversation with the special-teams coach like a request for high-level Pentagon clearance. In the way that most people in insular environments lose perspective, it is no different in NFL circles, where it can be easy to delude yourself into thinking that pro football is the most important thing in the world.

"I don't want a guy who's all hyped up," Zauner explains, when asked about the mental makeup of successful snappers he's coached. "Some of these kids—former linebackers and defensive ends—come in with the mentality that they're still going to be ultra-aggressive and bust people up." What Zauner is explaining is one of the tensions inherent in being a snapper. Football is a world in which you're told from an early age that you need to "get pissed off"; "get a chip on your shoulder"; and "be intense." But in fact, those are the very things that can derail a snapper. "It's almost like how you don't want a brain surgeon going into surgery all hyped up," he says.

"A lot of the good snappers have really laid-back, almost funny personalities," he says. "Snappers are an entirely different breed; it's like they have their own society within the game."

I ask Zauner how he coached snappers through rough patches, and his answer, though not terribly surprising, is a chilling reminder of the competitive nature of the NFL. His answer is that he basically never had to. "If you have a bad day as a snapper you're not going to be around long," he explains. "It's really going to make me wonder. In all my years of coaching I never had a guy snap the ball over a punter or holder's head in a game."

It's an interesting answer because it is essentially the "failure is not an option" approach, which seems to stand in stark contrast to the "but just relax and have fun" rhetoric that is often a part of coaching. It makes me further appreciate former New England Patriots snapper Brian Kinchen's brutal honesty in his book, which describes the self-doubt and struggles he faced in the days and hours leading up to the Super Bowl. It chronicles evenings spent snapping into pillows in his hotel room, trying to get his stroke right, and agonizing afternoons snapping erratically under the watchful gaze of head coach Bill Belichick, who may be pro football's current most intimidating man.

"If I see things going wrong, they're not gonna be my guy," Zauner adds. It occurs to me that coaching special teams at that level is less about developing talent and more about just collecting and curating it.

"Some coaches are just happy for a guy who can get the ball back there," he says.

But I always wanted to get a guy who could snap, block, and cover. When I was with the Vikings we had a guy, Mike Morris, who was a big guy who could snap well but didn't block great. When I got to the Ravens we had a guy named Joe Maese who couldn't block or cover, and the Ravens actually gave up some blocks on center stunts. Then we got Matt Katula who went on to lead the NFL in tackles. When I first started working with Matt he missed several tackles in a row, so I set up a drill for him. He would have to drag the bags out, set them up, and do this drill every Wednesday after practice; soon he wasn't missing tackles anymore. I saw him a few years later and asked him if he was still doing the drill, and he said "Hell no, that was a pain in the ass!"

I ask Zauner how he feels about the growing cottage industry that is snapping instruction—especially at the younger ages. And while he is a part of it, he realizes that his market niche is getting exposure for free agents and would-be NFL snappers. His camps are less about instruction and more about exposure at the highest level, because the NFL scouts and decision makers who attend trust his eye and evaluation.

"I think it's basically a good thing," he explains. "Provided the coaching is actually good. But I've seen some really bad coaching."

The nature of interviewing is to get somebody to try to answer a question honestly, but I find that the more of this I do, the more I want to lead subjects into territory they may not have considered before. For example, I see the scholarship-mill nature of the snapping-camp industry as something of a mixed blessing, in that it encourages hyper-specialization at a young age, which may preclude athletes from having other, more enriching, experiences. Simply put, it's not that fun to spend all of your high school and college years doing nothing but throwing a ball between your legs. Not to mention that rabidity and mania it breeds in parents, who swoon over the idea of little junior suiting up for Big Time State U. So, while I try to goad Zauner into having this conversation with me (because it will satisfy me), he's not going there. Instead, as is befitting of a special-teams coach, he thinks only of the improving quality of the snapping itself.

"As an NFL coach you can go out and buy a guy, but as a high school coach who's gonna be your snapper? I say give me ten guys who can throw a pass, doesn't matter what position they play. In five minutes I can break it down to four guys, and in another twenty I can teach those four how to snap. It's really like throwing a pass upside down."

On pressure: "I bring everybody around them to scream and holler. With snappers I'll take the red square dummies and hit them, just like they'll get hit in a game. I want them snapping in their pads, just like in a game. Some guys can snap in a T-shirt and shorts, but they struggle a little with pads on. And I'll put the stopwatch on them."

Regarding pressure, Zauner recently worked with former Green Beret and University of Texas snapper Nate Boyer, whose unlikely road to the NFL dream has been well documented. In short, Boyer is old (in his midthirties) and small (only 219 pounds). Still, he beat the odds to snap at one of the biggest college programs in the nation and is now trying to snap his way into the NFL. His recorded session at Zauner's senior combine is a little rough. He snaps high (at the facemask) and low (below the knees) on a few punt snaps. And while none of his field-goal snaps are unfieldable, some are a little low, and some lack the proper "laces" placement for which Zauner is (relatively, of course) famous.

I query Zauner on the importance of speed, for a snapper, and he explains that snapping, like real estate, is about "location, location, location." "I've cut the two fastest snappers I ever had," he says. "Because they were erratic. Most guys in the NFL are between .64 and .75. There was a guy named Nick Sundberg who went to the Panthers, and their punter wanted a slower snap. He started trying to take speed off of it, got a little erratic, and they kept the punter."

❊ ❊ ❊

It's been a few weeks since I've heard from my free-agent buddy Jon Akemon. No news might be good news, or no news might mean a sort of downward-swirling depression in which the number of days with no phone ringing begins to wear the lacquer off of one's good cheer and dreams. I worry that my friend is entering this stage, where each day it gets harder and harder to perpetuate the Dream.

I ask Akemon if he has heard anything from the FXFL. The last time we spoke, it was touch and go as to whether the upstart league would have the working capital to make a go at a second season.

"Yep," he says cryptically. I ask for a little more information. "Are you in?"

"Yep, I'm in," he says. "But I can't say which team because, besides Brooklyn, they're all gonna be new teams."

I smile, because Akemon is one step closer to his dream, and I'm one step closer to mine.

❊ ❊ ❊

Before getting his position with the Vikings, Zauner had a conversation with then head coach Dennis Green. "I want to hire you," said Green, to which Zauner replied, "Who makes the final decision on the kicker, punter, and snapper? Because that's gonna determine my success."

"Coaches, when making a decision on which job to take, need to know if they get the guys they want, and get the practice time they need."

Zauner was fortunate to work for a litany of coaches—Green, Dick Vermeil, George Allen, Brian Billick—for whom special teams was a priority. Our conversation eventually wanders to the current state of the NFL.

"This thing (Deflategate) with the Patriots is ridiculous," he says. Deflategate is, of course, a reference to Tom Brady's alleged deflation of several Patriot game balls in a 2014 playoff game against Indianapolis. Like many people in pro football, Zauner feels it's much ado about nothing—especially as a former special-teams coach, who has seen kickers manipulating the footballs since the beginning of time. Kickers are notorious for heating, cooling, compressing, massaging, and doing nearly everything that the laws of physics would allow to their footballs. "Everybody worked the ball." But nobody, necessarily, had a sense for how many pounds of pressure were in a given football at a given time.

"The suits are no longer football guys," Zauner explains. "They're into marketing . . . they're into making money. That's why the game is not like it used to be."

I ask Zauner if he misses the competitive environment of being on an NFL staff.

"I do miss the competitive environment," he says. "But I don't miss how coaching has changed. It's a league of general managers now, not coaches. You're not in control of a lot of things. Mike Ditka hired all of his coaches . . . he hired me. That would never fly today. I'm happiest when I'm coaching, and I'm coaching now. I get to see the players smile and improve. And I'm not driving my wife mad."

Long snapper Nate Boyer is a former U.S. Army Green Beret. *Courtesy of Nate Boyer.*

Boyer leads the Texas Longhorns onto the field, carrying the American flag. *Courtesy of Nate Boyer.*

Former Northern Illinois snapper and current snapping instructor Nolan Owen joined forces with longtime snapping instructor Chris Rubio. *Courtesy of Nolan Owen.*

Former **UCLA** long snapper Chris Rubio **(R)** has made a career of snapping instruction, and his camps are the conduit to a college scholarship for many young snappers. *Courtesy of Chris Rubio.*

Long snapper Jon Akemon bends over the football as a member of the FXFL's Hudson Valley Fort. *Courtesy of Jon Akemon.*

Akemon at Anderson (IN) University. *Courtesy of Jon Akemon.*

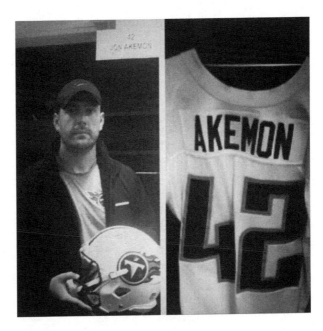

Akemon with Tennessee Titans helmet at minicamp. *Courtesy of Jon Akemon.*

Former San Diego State and Seattle Seahawks snapper Tyler Schmitt is now an accomplished landscape photographer. *Courtesy of Tyler Schmitt.*

Former NFL punter Glenn Pakulak now owns an apparel company called "Motown Over Yo'Town." *Courtesy of Glenn Pakulak.*

Glenn Pakulak warms up pregame as a member of the Oakland Raiders. *Courtesy of Glenn Pakulak.*

Longtime **NFL** special teams coach **Gary Zauner observes kicker Kevin Butler as a member of the Chicago Bears staff.** *Courtesy of Gary Zauner.*

Zauner with legendary coach George Allen at Long Beach State University. *Courtesy of Gary Zauner.*

The author enjoys a quiet moment pregame, as a member of the Windy City Ravens. *Courtesy of Ted Kluck.*

Walking down the tunnel, in the shadows. *Courtesy of Ted Kluck.*

Postgame, with son (and documentary photographer) Tristan Kluck. *Courtesy of Ted Kluck.*

Presnap at the Mobile, Alabama, tryout—a jumble of nerves. *Courtesy of Ted Kluck.*

With family after a game in France, as a member of the **St. Brieuc Licornes.** *Courtesy of Ted Kluck.*

10

THE PRIVATE LESSON
Nolan Owen Part 2

Nolan Owen's workout facility is tucked away in an industrial park north of East Dundee, Illinois, which is itself northwest of the city of Chicago and has, like many other small towns in the area, been engulfed and eventually choked by the suburban sprawl that is this entire area. When I walk into the warehouse, I'm greeted by Owen and his business partner Nick Adams (whose parents must have been Hemingway fans). The diminutive Adams was the starting long snapper at Central Michigan University. Both men are shortish and lack the traditional presence and stature one usually associates with top-of-the-physical-gene-pool Division I athletes.

This space has the kind of ethos that has become standard in the suburban-training-facility market. There are buckets of protein powders available for purchase. There are tires available for flipping, and all manner of other "private training" apparatus available for the breaking down and eventually building back up of suburban athletes.

This stuff is expensive. Depending on the instructor, an hour of football training (to be clear, these aren't Owen's prices) can run between $150 and $200, with the prices ratcheting up as additional hours are purchased. Comprehensive personal training "packages" can run well over a thousand dollars.

Of course, the snapping-training subculture is merely a drop in the proverbial bucket compared to the kinds of dollars being shelled out by the parents of young quarterbacks. There are countless websites touting "Quarterback Training and Development," all of which promise some version of the same thing: cutting-edge training that will allow a quarterback to matriculate to the magical Next Level. All of the sites have basically the same pictures of the same lantern-jawed genetically awesome quarterbacks looking steely eyed and laser focused in much the same ways. The amount of money flowing through this industry is astonishing. Gone are the days of throwing the ball on an empty field with your friends in the summer. Being a young football player, today, is a full-time gig.

There are quarterback camps and private sessions available for "players" in grades 4–6, for people who were previously known as children. There's an organization that boasts the "nation's only dedicated curriculum for youth QB development!" Quarterbacks can access an "unlimited year of 'Beach Training' for only $500!"[1] One quarterback instructor claims to have been playing and studying the game of football since the age of five, causing me to wonder what this in-depth study looked like, at five.

All of this has the aggregate effect of making me feel very cynical about the private-training circuit, because of how manifestly unfun it seems. Granted, there is the appearance of fun—and coaches in this space are savvy enough to create T-shirts and a "family" and a "culture" around their particular brand of training. The rock-and-a-hard-place dilemma for parents, about this, is the idea that if they don't shell out for private training, their son will "fall behind," a concept that caters to our most basic insecurities as people. God forbid we fall behind! But what "falling behind" really entails is the reality of not being good enough, which has been around since the beginning of time. The fact of the matter is that I could have had all of the private training in the world and probably still would have topped out right around where I topped out. There's the very real possibility that private training is succeeding as an industry only because of the very real fear that everybody else is doing it.

Contrasted with this are the stories of the old generation of athletes, including guys such as Jim Kelly, who became great by throwing a bunch of passes to his dad and brothers in the backyard, and playing basketball and baseball when it wasn't football season. Or there's Walter Payton dancing and playing the drums and running up and down levees like a maniac just because he thought it would make him great. I want to believe that somebody can still become great, even if they don't specialize at age five. The focus, in all this rampant specialization and boutique training, is that "what you're doing"—whether it's throwing footballs in the water, flipping a tire, or hooking up to some virtual-reality machine—is somehow different or revolutionary. But by the looks of it, everybody is doing pretty much the same thing; the point is that they're doing it because they all feel they have to do it.

But is football any more joyful, and are our memories any more significant, because of this? For every athlete who gets to the Next Level because of his boutique training, there are probably hundreds more whose parents have effectively just flushed the money. When I get all wistful and romantic vis-à-vis high school football, what I get wistful and romantic about isn't the opportunities I had to play in college or even the nice camps my folks sent me to. It's the town, the lights, the band's drumbeats, and the looks on my teammates' faces in the locker room and in the huddle. None of us were our own franchises, yet we still had aspirations that included each other.

Soon I am stretching on a prickly carpet of old-school AstroTurf with Owen and hearing him explain in no uncertain terms that it is no longer good enough to simply snap well on film for your high school team.

"So say I'm a really good high school snapper with good film. Is that enough to get me a scholarship?" I ask.

"No," he says flatly. "It's not enough. A snapper needs to be ranked and validated by someone else." The someone else, of course, being Chris Rubio or (he hopes) Nolan Owen. "College coaches need to know that you can snap perfectly in every situation," he explains. "And you have to be able to talk about why a snap is bad, when it's bad. It's not enough to just say 'I don't know.'"

There's something both authoritarian and perhaps even a little defensive about Owen's tone, as though my wide-eyed disbelief that snapping has become the ultra-specialized cottage industry that it is somehow invalidates what he does. It doesn't (invalidate). I'm really impressed—shocked but impressed. What's happening in long snapping is, in part, a microcosm of what's happening more broadly in all of sport—the suburbanization and specialization of certain positions. More bluntly, only a certain type of kid can afford the Rubio/Owen camp circuit and private instruction gamut that it takes to get "ranked," which is the pipeline to the holy grail of the college scholarship—a holy grail that is grail-like for this demographic more because of what it represents than even what it even provides monetarily. The ability to say "My kid is on scholarship at _____," is a big deal for which parents are willing to shell out a shocking amount of money on the front end.

The populist in me bristles at this a little, and maybe this is why Owen seems a little defensive. I've always kind of exalted football as the ultimate meritocracy—a place where your bravery, talent, and drive is always rewarded, regardless of socioeconomic status. Stories of this kind of achievement are a part of the story and mythos of football through the ages. In fact, it is a part of the mythos of the city of Chicago, where George Halas took an industrial team at a corn products factory (the Decatur Staleys) and from it created the National Football League. It is the ultimate rags-to-riches narrative. This budding industry suggests otherwise, and by that I mean the idea that if a suburbanite child has enough money and enough rides to private lessons, he can become a ranked and viable college long-snapping prospect. But I guess the up-side is great snapping at nearly every level.

"You're in the right place geographically for this," I explain to Owen, as we discuss the traffic and population explosion in the area. Nick Adams explains that he is opening a franchise in the metro Detroit area, which is experiencing a similar suburban boom.

For the boutique snapping coach, the ranking is really the bargain-ing chip with which camp and private lesson fees are wheedled out of football-hungry suburban parents. The rankings and evaluations are giv-en to colleges for free. Owen's other company, the National Long Snap-ping Association, is, like Rubio, in the business of doling out ratings, and to his credit, the process seems relatively scientific. Snap accuracy is measured on the percentage of snaps that hit between the punter's numbers and knees, and snap times are measured on a scale between .650 seconds and faster, down to .781 seconds.

Snappers are also evaluated on height, weight, forty time, and even grade-point average, and ultimately snappers are assimilated into a da-tabase that college coaches can parse according to their own criteria. Based on my height (six foot three), weight (248ish), speed in college (4.95), and GPA, I would rate highly. I'm fairly certain that my snaps would time well on the stopwatch too. But for me, consistency is the killer. It's what would keep me from the coveted five-star rating. "The five-star athlete is a lock to snap at the D1 level," he explains. "He should receive multiple scholarship offers. The four-star player is worthy of preferred walk-on status and partial scholarship offers. In the history of our company, we've only ever had one snapper get a five-star rating," he explains.

All snappers are rated by committee, by Owen and his business partners Kyle Stelter and Matt Wigley, both of whom have significant college or pro experience. The path to a college snapping scholarship now seems both abundantly clear and hopelessly complicated.

"You need to go to, on average, nine camps in order to get a ranking," Owen explains. "You figure the camp fee, travel, lodging . . . it adds up to about a thousand bucks per camp." What's still interesting, though, is that when one flips on the television on a Saturday afternoon, Florida State's defense, by and large, isn't populated by kids from Aurora and Bolingbrook and East Dundee, which is a nice way of saying that white athletes are figuring out a way to get a place at the table in Big Time College Football. It's just a way that costs some money.

❀ ❀ ❀

We are surrounded in the warehouse by a variety of vintage and modern training implements including rope ladders (for quick feet), tractor tires (for flipping), and giant, thick, nautical-type ropes (to build shoulder strength). These are the tools of the modern suburban trainer's trade and the tools for which the modern suburban parent will pay top dollar. Owen shares the facility with a former Northern Illinois University (NIU) teammate turned speed coach.

Over the course of the next ninety minutes, Owen will take something that for me has always been about talent and feel, and make it scientific. At the Owen school of long snapping, there is a reason for everything that goes wrong in a long snap, and there is a way to fix it. Whereas before a coach would simply say, "Can anybody snap?" at the beginning of fall practice, today (theoretically) if one implements the physics involved in the Owen/Rubio methods, anyone can snap consistently every time.

We start with some simple catch drills (including one called the "forehead" drill), revealing that I'm not fully snapping my wrists at the end of each snap and so robbing my ball of precious spiraling rotations that keep it cutting through the midwestern wind and weather. "If you don't go 'fingertips to forearms' your ball will wobble," Owen explains. "There's a lot going on with your hands," he adds, meaning that there's a lot that's wrong.

Owen isn't at all a jerk about any of this at all; he's a really nice guy, and there is a ton that I still don't know about snapping. But in football there is a de jure and de facto pecking order, and you have to achieve your way to the top of it. And until you do, you'll probably be condescended to.

Football is all about hierarchies. It's one of the most interesting aspects of guy-on-guy relationships: the pecking order and how certain guys always need to be at the top of it even though what they've done is already pretty impressive. Generally, I'm happy to let whomever I'm with sit atop whatever real or perceived pecking order exists in their mind. It's just easier that way. Another guy-on-guy, competitive rhetorical device is asking questions to which you probably don't know the answer, in order to reaffirm pecking order. Instead of just giving the information, a coach will sometimes frame it as questions, as if to remind me of all that I don't know. It "works" in the sense that it does remind me that he is the expert, but still, it's not exactly my favorite.

We then do a drill in which I deep-bend my knees twice before actually snapping—a motion that's supposed to help my body remember to lock out my knees, thus providing maximum power. I can feel it working and feel the steps beginning to come together.

He sets up a camera and films me from three different angles, so that every bad snapping habit I have developed over thirty-plus years is laid out in painstaking, slow-motion detail.

Then I actually snap some footballs to Owen, and he begins the videotaped work of breaking down every aspect of my stance and delivery. I snapped fairly well in my sample snaps (save for one bad one), but there was still much work to do. Like most old-school snappers, my butt was too high in the air, resulting in a football that has a tendency to sometimes drift high. Owen drops my hips, opens my knees, and forces me to puff out my chest. It feels awkward—more like a birth stance than a football stance—but soon I'm seeing the method in his madness. When I lock out my knees during the snap, the upward pop of my back generates an incredible amount of power. And widening the knees allows my elbows to fully rotate through, meaning that I'm getting full extension and power. The wrist snap puts the finishing touches on the spiral. The physics behind it really make sense.

"You need to move your guide hand down," he says, of the left hand that usually rests near the top of the football. "Where would you put a fat guy in a canoe?" he asks. It is one of those questions that are dependent upon a not immediately obvious answer for an unrelated problem. "In the middle," I reply.

"Right, but why?"

"Because in the front or the back he would tip the canoe," I say, understanding what he's getting at.

"When your guide hand is too far up the football, it has a tendency to tail up," he says. "Too far down and it tails down. You lose power and speed. Timing is everything."

In time I will lay on my back on the turf, practicing the fingertips-to-forearms method, and while Owen's ball spirals tightly and returns right back to his hands, mine is all over the place. But again, when I bend back over the ball to finish the workout with a few snaps to Owen, I feel more comfortable and confident.

"I have a drill sheet with over two hundred drills on it," he explains.

I indicate that I would love to see it.

"You wouldn't understand any of it," he says, though it is oddly inoffensive—sort of like being told by your college chemistry professor that you wouldn't understand his graduate-level research. He's right. I probably wouldn't.

11

THE RUBIO CAMP

Best Buy. Target. Jewel-Osco. Buffalo Wild Wings. Best Buy. Target. Jewel-Osco. Buffalo Wild Wings. This is the mise-en-scène of the west Chicago suburbs as I wind my way toward Aurora Central Catholic High School and Chris Rubio's Chicago snapping camp. Traffic crawls along, and there is nothing to differentiate one suburb from another. "You must lose your personhood to this, at some level," I explain to my father on the phone (although talking on the phone while driving is technically illegal in Illinois). "In the sense that being from Plainfield is now no different than being from Lockport or Minooka or Mooseheart or Oswego. They're completely indiscernible."

My dad grew up in Plainfield when it used to be a sleepy farm community and has seen it transform year by year into the suburb it is today, complete with the aforementioned chain places and the quaint gentrified main street that is obligatory in each of these hamlets, otherwise known as the location of your daughter's dance studio and the overpriced hipster burger place.

Rubio, like Nolan Owen, knows where his current and future clients are located, and on this day, the grass field at Aurora Central Catholic is abuzz with activity. As I wheel into the parking lot I can see balls flying through the air and a variety of kids from eighth grade through college age, all hunched over learning the art and science of snapping. Within minutes, it's clear why Rubio is so good at this, as he's equal parts football coach and tent-revival preacher. The guy is entertaining, and the camp is a really perfectly paced mix of instruction, games, competition, and Rubio talking.

He is passionate about snapping as a specialty endeavor and has no particular qualms about players specializing as snappers. He addressed a common question on his blog: why not just have another position player—like a center—snap for punts and kicks? Rubio, a good-natured guy, blew a gasket.

"Rarely, and I mean *rarely*, do I get fired up about something, but the above question seriously upsets me," he wrote. "The more that Rubio Long Snapping grows and the more that Rubio Long Snappers get picked up for college, the more you will hear/read/see people that think they know what they are talking about in regards to football and Long Snappers."

These "experts" might be on Twitter, Facebook, and blogs all over the country spraying their "wisdom" to anyone that will swallow it. And 99.9 percent of the time it is *really, really* ignorant.

"Asking a lineman to become a Long Snapper is like asking a seventies Cadillac El Dorado to drive like a 2015 Ferrari. They are two completely different types of machines meant to do two completely different things . . . kinda like a lineman and a Long Snapper."

Everyone is here for dream-related reasons—because the specialization of the long snapper now allows a kid who isn't freakishly huge or athletic the "right" to dream about a college or NFL career. Now, don't get me wrong, elite snappers at the pro level are still freakishly athletic and mentally strong but in a different, and more accessible, way. These parents and their children see the Rubio camp as a pipeline to those dreams—as a way to walk through the door that has been opened by the specialty snapper. And Rubio, for all his work with college-eligible snappers, has put his stamp on the NFL as well, as the following Rubio snappers have been on NFL rosters or received NFL minicamp invites:

Carson Tinker—Jacksonville Jaguars
Justin Drescher—New Orleans Saints
Jon Weeks—Houston Texans
Aaron Brewer—Denver Broncos
Tyler Schmitt—Seattle Seahawks
Christian Yount—Cleveland Browns
Nick Sundberg—Washington Redskins
Rick Lovato—Green Bay Packers

Joe Cardona—New England Patriots
Andrew East—Seattle Seahawks
Nate Boyer—Seattle Seahawks
Corey Adams—Dallas Cowboys
Chris Maikranz—Houston Texans
Drew Ferris—New York Jets
Drew Howell—Tampa Bay Buccaneers

It is a strange July day in the Chicago area, meaning that it is fifty-nine degrees and sprinkling. The parents who aren't on the field with their kids are sitting in folding chairs, swaddled in blankets. Rubio is in his element, stalking about in his ubiquitous nineties sunglasses. The parents are eating this up. Laughter ensues often.

"My advice to the parents is to be supportive of your sons," wrote former Rubio and University of Nebraska long snapper Gabriel Miller on Rubio's blog.

> Your son is embarking on one of the toughest journeys in all of sports, and that is to get a scholarship for long snapping and playing college football. This adds a ton of pressure to his already hectic life as a teenager, so the biggest thing you could do is support him during this crazy time. There were times when it seemed life was ending because I wasn't getting where I wanted in my long snapping, but my parents supported me and gave me confidence that if I continued to work hard the results would follow. And at the time I was given a full-ride scholarship from the University of Nebraska and ranked as the number 2 long snapper in my class, there was no one I wanted to share that moment with more than with my parents who had supported me during the whole process.

That, I think, is the endearing thing about the Rubio camp experience. Rather than being grim, joyless, and cutthroat, it seems almost nurturing. The parents are on the field often, working with their sons and enjoying the experience together. I'm reminded that the best thing about football—and really the only enduring thing of value—was sharing it with my dad. However, it's just common sense that in the grand numbers game that is college football, only a small percentage of these families will get what they want—and hopefully there is something more, something intrinsic, to be "gotten" from this.

"If I shove the ball up your butt and you fart it out, that's where it'll go!" Rubio shouts, underscoring some point about ball placement. More laughter. Where you want the ball, on a punt snap, is somewhere between the punter's midthigh and the middle of his ribcage. To wit, from the Rubio blog:

> The Rubio Zone is *exactly* where the Long Snapper should hit the punter for best accuracy on a punt snap. The Rubio Zone is from the punter's midthigh to his lowest rib and no wider than their armpits. Anything above the lowest rib could cause the punter to turn his hands over which will force him to flip them back over to punt the ball. Anything below the punter's midthigh will cause the punter to bend and that could throw off their timing. Anything outside of the armpits will force the punter to step one way or the other.
> The Rubio Zone is the perfect location and what every Long Snapper should try to hit on every single snap. Anything outside of the Rubio Zone will negatively impact your overall snap time, as well as total get off time (snap, catch, and punt).

I'm startled to find that the parents don't look much older than me, though they are here with their kids (normal), and I am here because I'm still trying to snap (not normal). When I arrive, the campers are circled around two bigger kids in the middle, playing a "burnout"-type game where they are snapping as hard as they can at each other from a distance of ten yards. They look young, but they're snapping rockets. One of them looks exactly like a young Conan O'Brien, and the other one is decked out in Notre Dame gear from head to toe and is, in fact, Notre Dame's starting long snapper Scott Daly.

I soon discover that the kid with the Conan O'Brien look is Taybor Pepper, a senior-to-be at Michigan State University, where he has been the starting long snapper for coach Mark Dantonio. Pepper, from Saline, Michigan, was ranked among the nation's top snappers by Chris Rubio and was a three-year starting snapper at Saline High School. His dad played offensive guard at Illinois during the Jeff George era. Pepper came to Michigan State with a gaunt 185 pounds on his six-foot-five frame but is now a solid 235.

"We've probably been to fifty camps," explains his mother, Donna Pepper. "We started at the end of eighth grade at the Dallas camp and have gone every season. We've been to every Vegas event."

I ask her why she's been so loyal to the Rubio brand, though I'm guessing it has something to do with the kind of community that forms in wandering tribes like this.

"He learned a lot and got the tools to practice at home," she explains. "We liked what other parents were saying." As we talk there is a flying drone camera buzzing overhead; it is a constant throughout the day at the Rubio camp, reminding the boys that every rep is being filmed for posterity and review. But the other thing about the drone—whether or not the drone footage ever gets "reviewed" or "broken down" in a football sense—is that it adds a sense of gravitas to the whole thing. There's a sense that having cameras around is good because things that are perpetually filmed, such as this, are perceived as "big time."

"When Taybor was in eighth grade his coach made everyone get down and snap, and he showed some talent for it," Donna says. "I started searching online for long-snapping instruction, and Rubio was the second coach I called. He was very patient with me and spent thirty or forty minutes with me on the phone answering all my questions. Over the years we became an unspoken community . . . all of the parents still talk, and the boys keep in touch. One of them, Reid Ferguson, was first team All-American at LSU last year. Taybor was second team."

While we talk, Rubio produces a camp toilet in order to illustrate how a snapper must get his butt down in the stance. Again, this draws laughs, and it is a tried and true Rubio camp joke, but it works to illustrate the point he's making. And more broadly, he is taking something boring and technical and making it fun, which is what good teachers in any discipline do. Many college professors don't know how to do this, and education suffers for it. Not that all instruction is entertainment, but in this context it helps a lot.

He accidentally knocks Pepper to the ground after a snapping demo, drawing a yell from his mother. "Hey Rubio, he has a season to play soon!"

"The most important thing we learned here was how to navigate the waters of recruiting and choosing a college," she explains. "Back then there weren't many snappers getting scholarships. But then Scott [Daly, Notre Dame] got his offer. Taybor had a lot of preferred walk-on offers and was actually committed to the University of Michigan, but then Michigan State had an off-the-field issue with their snapper and coach

Dantonio called to offer Taybor a scholarship. MSU was always his first choice."

What's interesting about Pepper is that football wasn't his dream as it is for many, and as it was for me. "Taybor wasn't really a sports kid," she says. "He was always more up for reading a book. His dad, who works in athletic administration, offered to throw a birthday party for him in the college locker room when he was in grade school, and he said, 'Why would I want that?' He just didn't grasp how cool it was." Indeed, according to Pepper's Spartan athletics biography, he didn't play another position at Saline and only ran track as a sophomore. Pepper's day job, since eighth grade, has been snapping a football.

He was thrown immediately into the fray as a Spartan, when MSU's starting snapper was injured in a diving accident. Pepper—the 185-pound freshman—started on national television against Boise State. Both teams were ranked in the top ten. "I was so nervous," Donna Pepper recalls. "ESPN's sideline reporter did a story on how Dantonio stole Taybor away from Michigan." On the clip, Pepper points excitedly into the stands after snapping successfully on his first college field-goal attempt. He looks tiny at 185 pounds—even the helmet looks too big for him.

Pepper was a rarity in that he played for the same head coach his entire career. Stories abound about one of Rubio's core commandments: don't pick a school based on the coach or the coaching staff. A kid who committed to one coaching staff could end up playing for two head coaches and three special-teams coordinators before his career is over. A quick glance at any coach's bio reveals the fact that a bag is always packed—coaching is a nomadic endeavor that means selling a house and packing up the family every few years. But I remember, even from my recruiting adventures in the mid-nineties, how easy it is to become attached to a certain coach, whose job it is to come into your living room and woo everyone in your family.

"Now we're starting to interview agents,"[1] Donna explains, as Taybor enters his senior season as a top NFL snapping prospect. "It's a weird, full-circle kind of thing, as I remember going through it with my husband after he graduated." Given that Taybor wasn't a sports freak as a kid, I wonder if the NFL is really his dream.

"Oh, it definitely is now," she says. "He eats and sleeps it. But there are so few jobs each year, and we don't necessarily want to go with an agent who is representing multiple snappers in that job market. But we want somebody who has placed specialists on NFL rosters. We know that almost anybody can negotiate a contract, but the marketing piece—being able to market the player to teams—is most important."

The camp motors on around us, as in one corner of the field, kids are filming their profiles and in another quadrant snappers and punters are now working together. I see, on the parents, an endless parade of school names and sweatshirts that I recognize. There is a woman from Grand Ledge, Michigan, my current hometown, and even one from Mississinewa High School in Indiana, one of my former rivals.

"Hey, are you guys from Gas City?" I ask the woman in the Mississinewa Indians sweatshirt. The Indians (a moment to appreciate the political incorrectness of their name) were always cheap, dirty, tough poor kids from a really rough little town. Just like us. Though as I reflect on that now, there is more admiration than contempt. I enjoyed playing against them, even though they were the types of kids who would twist your ankle in a pile.

Like nearly all central Indiana folks they turn out to be almost disarmingly friendly. We chat for a long time about the conference, the football woes at my school (Blackford), the local economy (grim and dismal), and their son, who is a rising star on the Rubio camp circuit. He'll be a junior this season and has already been to big camps, including one at Indiana University. I am reminded of my recruiting trip to Indiana with my dad—a defining moment.

"He wants something bigger," his mom explains. "And he wants to leave Indiana." I can relate to both of these emotions. I shake the boy's hand. He is a thick, low-slung little guy who is all hips and thighs, and an unkempt head of hair. He has the hardened look of the Indiana farm kid. He has the football, tough-guy sneer down pat. I immediately like him and want to see him conquer this, if it's what he wants.

The camp is breaking up for lunch, and Donna Pepper is talking with me about watching her kids grow up. "I'm redoing Taybor's room now . . . and was starting to paint the ceiling when I noticed a smudge on it, in exactly the shape of the nose of the football. It's where he'd been laying on his back, working on technique, night after night. It makes me sad to think that it's almost over. I don't want to paint over it."

12

TRANSITION

Tennessee, Glenn Pakulak, and Jon Akemon

"Let me tell you something about Jonathan Akemon," explains former NFL punter and current actor Glenn Pakulak.

> I met Jonathan when he was a kid trying to walk on to the Kentucky football team. This was a guy who had limited athletic ability, and no idea how to really snap the football. He would lift it up like two feet off the turf and just kind of sling it back there. But nobody out-worked this kid. He worked so hard, and he hustled and networked and for him to have been in a Titans camp . . . man . . . it's unbeliev-able . . . and just proof of what can happen when you work hard and don't let anything stop you.

Positive energy emanates from Pakulak. Within minutes of convers-ing on the phone, you realize he's the friend you've always wanted: encouraging, supportive, and always upbeat, while at the same time being completely honest about his postfootball struggles. Despite his impressive array of acting-related Instagram photos, he is disarmingly real. Regarding the Instagram photos—there are shots of Glenn in his high school football gear, in which he looks like you always wanted to look in high school—like the James Van Der Beek character in *Varsity Blues*. There are shots of him about town, in Los Angeles, with a variety of amazing-looking people. There are posed publicity-type acting shots and unplanned candids—though in both cases, one thing is startlingly clear: this is a ridiculously photogenic individual.

Pakulak's story is similar to Akemon's. Born in Pontiac, Michigan, he grew up in rural Lapeer, where he excelled as a football, baseball, and basketball player. After two years at tiny Rochester College, a National Association of Intercollegiate Athletics (NAIA) school where he played baseball and basketball, he walked onto the football team at the University of Kentucky. He paid his own way for two years and initially played on the junior varsity. Pakulak, the product of hardworking blue-collar parents, hadn't made the rounds of the summer beauty pageants that are modern-day specialty camps. He just played all over the football field and kicked the heck out of the ball when he got the opportunity.

"I was lost those first couple of years at Kentucky, wondering what I was doing down there at times," says Pakulak. "So I just lifted. A lot." Eventually the hard work paid off, as Pakulak acquired a reputation for headhunting return men as well as booming punts. Despite being chosen All-SEC over punters like Dustin Colquitt (Tennessee) and Donnie Jones (LSU), and ranked as the second best punter in the nation by NFL draft guru Mel Kiper, he went undrafted—thus setting off a long, strange football odyssey.

"Glenn is a very passionate guy, and kind of like a mentor to me," says Akemon. "I was going to walk on and let a lot of stuff get into my head." Akemon met Pakulak when he was considering walking onto the Kentucky football team. That opportunity never materialized, but the two have stayed in close contact ever since. Akemon counts Pakulak as his closest friend, even as he ponders the end of his football dream.

"Football is something I'm very passionate about," Akemon says. "I've loved this game more than I've loved my family at times. But in all actuality you have to move on at the end of the day. There are so many guys who played in high school and college who express a desire and hold onto that for years and years and years."

Pakulak held onto his dream for years, and it finally came true in 2008 when he suited up in his first regular season game with the New Orleans Saints. Before that, it was lots of invitations for tryouts, mini-camps, training camps, and even a stint in NFL Europe where he lived and played in Amsterdam. He was told to see the coach and bring his playbook eight times, meaning that he made eight calls to parents and girlfriends telling them that he was headed home on a lonely flight. He spent time with the Seahawks, Steelers, Falcons, and Bears, and two stints each with the Raiders and Titans. He worked a litany of odd jobs to make ends meet in between.

"People see that I've spent nine years doing pro football stuff and assume that I must be loaded," he explains. "It's not true. I probably made $350,000 total in all those years, but you add up all the travel and training and times without income . . . it goes pretty fast."

"I'm not a cocky guy, Ted, but I'm sure about what I am really good at," he explains. "Al Davis, who made all the decisions in Oakland until he was on his deathbed, knew punters. He drafted Ray Guy in the first round and Shane Lechler (who has the highest average in the history of the NFL). Al signed me there in 06, 08, and 11. Shane was there all those years and will go down as one of the top three punters in the history of the NFL. I punted with him every day, and it boggled his mind every year that I was back in Oakland for preseason with him and not another team's punter. So much so that he was inches away from walking me into his super agent's office, Tom Condon, one of the most powerful agents in all of sports. I didn't press the issue; a week later I was released after the preseason and so it never happened."

As I talk to Glenn, and we share a similar, borderline awkward passion for all things vintage, it becomes clear that the 2008 season with New Orleans was something of a watershed. It was the golden year. I ask him if all the struggle was worth it.

"Every bit of it," he says. "It's made me who I am." I am, truthfully, a little disappointed. I've been waiting a long time for somebody to admit that it wasn't worth it. "I've met some great people along the way and everything as far as playing happens to fast! It's so surreal . . . almost like this fictional story is taking place with all these people watching. You are kind of just there. Hard to explain. You've gotta dial those anxious feelings back real quick though, or a mucky substance is likely to start running down the back of your leg!"

Perhaps that is what makes a great specialist: not the absence of anxiety, which would be inhuman, but the ability to rein it in and dial it back. Pakulak then tells an amazing story, about his first NFL game in his hometown of Detroit.

"When I was with the Saints we came to play the Lions a week before Christmas," he recalls. "I bought fifty tickets . . . spent 3,200 bucks." Pakulak arrived at Ford Field, probably through the typical Detroit slate-gray snow and sleet, to find his white NFL visitor's jersey in a gleaming locker at the new facility, which is fashioned after an old-timey Detroit street, harkening back to better economic times for that struggling city. The field is bathed in natural light, and he probably warmed up joyfully, booming punts into the factory-like rafters, all the while searching the blue stadium seats for his throng of admirers. It was a watershed life moment set to a soundtrack of arena hip-hop, the realization of a dream, and a victory lap. And then the unthinkable happened.

"We went 13-for-13 on third down that day and won 42–0," he explains. "I didn't punt once! In the locker room after the game, Coach [Sean] Payton brought the team together, made the announcement, and threw me the game ball! Bradshaw talked about it on Fox after the game."

I share the anecdote with my wife who, thoughtfully, wonders if there's something to be learned about premature celebration in that story. "You're asking the wrong guy," I tell her. I am, in fact, phobic of celebrating—prematurely or otherwise. I'm the guy who after seven years of teaching at the same university was still afraid to buy a sweat-shirt, for fear that things might go south.

Pakulak was cut shortly thereafter and, after stints with the Jets, Redskins, and Chargers, was out of football in 2010. "I was starting my life over at age thirty-two," he says. "I wasn't going to go out and get some job selling medical equipment like a lot of my friends. I could have made a nice living, had my weekends off to do whatever I wanted. But I want to do something I'm passionate about."

Like many aspiring actors, he migrated west to Los Angeles, where he spent 1,200 bucks a month on four hundred square feet. It was a struggle and a grind.

"I would just lift all the time in college and went from 185 in high school up to 230 pounds and jacked. It's brutal in acting, in that I've had to burn forty-five pounds of muscle off my body just to get jobs as an actor. My body was so accustomed to being big for so long so that I don't have to lift to stay jacked. I just eat right and run all the time."

It got so challenging in LA that Pakulak was forced to sell off some of his vintage clothing collection. Vintage is a way of life for the ex-punter. "When I played I drove around a flawless '85 Fleetwood Caddy with ten thousand original miles that I got from my grandpa. The brothers would go *wild*! I was known as 'Old School' and 'Pakillac' in New Orleans." He expresses a desire to find a pair of fifties-vintage football boots on eBay, file off the cleats, and wear them as everyday boots. I explain that my personal eBay holy grail was a pair of vintage Pony nub AstroTurf shoes.

"I know exactly what those are!" he says. "*So* clean! Let's just get together, bromance, and talk vintage all day long." I explain that we sound gayer than Siegfried and Roy, to which he responds, "Nah, we're more vintage gay, like Larry and Balky."

❊ ❊ ❊

Shortly after connecting with Glenn, I hear from Jon Akemon, who is nearing the end of his shift driving a beverage delivery truck. I make out his southern Indiana drawl (which is different than Texas drawl or Deep-South drawl) over the roar of his delivery truck's engine.

"Me and Glenn are pretty close man . . . I told him about all the people reaching out to me looking for gigs when I got into the NFL. He said he was trying to get this book stuff together, and it's really hard to find a literary agent." I explain that I'm glad to introduce Glenn to my agent and glad to do whatever I can to help either of them out. I know the lostness that sets in after football. I have been battling it myself for years.

"Glenn was booming punts the last time he played; I think it was with the Saints. After the season they gave up a draft pick for a punter and let him go. Glenn's had some rough times. He'd be on a team for five or six games and then get cut."

I ask Akemon about the team that was going to sign him before the draft. It's a topic he has been hesitant to broach, keeping it shrouded in secrecy when it was happening and not bringing it up since.

I ask him about the FXFL, and the all-star game in New Zealand. Though I can sense his mood, regarding football, starting to change. There is a maturation process happening in Jon. He's starting to think in terms of "if" not "when." Gone are the statements of bravado, having been replaced by a sober and more grown-up perspective on life and reality. Football people may see this as weakness. I see it as a strength—as my friend growing up.

"New Zealand is pretty much locked, for sure," he says, of an all-star game that has the telltale look of something ill-fated and destined to fail. The New Zealand concept involves getting former NFL coaches involved—Mike Holmgren is reportedly attached—and rosters full of young guys who have spent time in NFL camps. Why the game is happening in New Zealand is anybody's guess. "That's pretty much gonna be the last go-around if nothing happens from that or the FXFL. There's a lot more to life man, and I don't want to miss out on having a family."

Speaking of family, I let Akemon know that I need to go in order to get my twelve-year-old son off to football practice. We've recently moved to west Tennessee for a faculty position at a university for me, and it seems as if it's 150 degrees with 100 percent humidity all the time here, like constantly running a low-grade fever. Tristan arrived in town and immediately started football on a new team at a new school. And he wanted me to teach him to snap. I groaned a little bit inwardly, knowing the agony that would await him, but then remembered that he is a far better athlete than I am, both physically and mentally. And being that he's a seventh grader on a team comprised primarily of eighth graders, it may be just the thing to get him on the field.

He worked through the initial awkwardness and frustration, and after a few sessions is firing lasers. His punt snaps, if not lightning fast, are usually on target. His field-goal snaps are fast and perfect. Like his father, he feels confident there. "This could be your ticket onto the field this season," I explain. "And if you do this well . . . you never know. It's a good way to go to college."

Even as the words cross my lips, I hate myself for saying them. Given the short time I spent as a college athlete, and all of the time I have spent around elite athletes as a writer, there's a large part of me that doesn't even want Tristan to play college football, because of the idolatry and lack of perspective it breeds. It's also just a grind involving many tedious hours of weight training, film study, therapy sessions in the training room, and head-on collisions on the field. On one level, I'd love for my sweet son to avoid all of this, and to just be able to go to college as a "regular" kid—meeting a diverse group of friends and being stimulated by his studies. After football ended for me in college, my entire world opened up, as I met kids who wanted to talk about more than just football and wanted to do more than just sit in their rooms playing Madden. There was a time when I thought being a regular kid meant death. I remember telling my parents that I didn't even want to *be* in college without football. But the truth is, being a regular kid was the best thing that ever happened to me.

Tristan returns from practice and informs me that he is taking reps at quarterback. There is a particular combination of elation and misery that comes with the office of Quarterback's Father. You'll find this man either along the top row of the bleachers, standing alone, or perhaps pacing by himself along the fence because, as they say in other overly dramatic situations, it's lonely at the top.

That said, I coached my son for several years and he never played quarterback for me. He was a battering ram of a fullback and a heat-seeking missile of a linebacker but never the quarterback, never the guy who has his hands on the football on every play. It took moving ten hours south, joining a new school, and starting football the day we moved into town for all of that to happen. And we didn't ask for any of it. There was no politicking; there were no films shared via e-mail with the coach and really no dialogue with the coach at all. This (not interfacing with the coach) has been pure joy, being that we just moved out of a "Daddyball" community where every father wore lots of UnderArmour gear and was very heavily involved. There were lots of dads waiting along the fence row by the practice field, and starting a lot of sentences with their sons' coaches with the phrase, "I don't mean to tell you how to do your job, but . . ."

Regarding the coach, he is right out of Southern Football Coach central casting: big, lumbering, yells a lot, runs long practices, runs three plays total, and probably has a shrine to Paul "Bear" Bryant in the narthex of his home.

Regarding being the quarterback's father, when your son plays a regular position such as fullback or middle linebacker, you don't have the conflicting emotions of dread and excitement on every single play. There is the vague sense that he could make a great play, or make a mistake, but with a quarterback, those are multiplied tenfold. My son started his first game as the seventh-grade quarterback last night, and after a few plays I was by myself, pacing along a fence. We were playing against a very tony, upscale ten-thousand-dollars-a-year private school that may or may not have been built to avoid racial integration in our metro area's school system. The officiating crew appeared to have been alumni of said school. Their field was nicer than any grass field I ever played on at any level of football. It had a manicured hedgerow around it, and walking on it felt like walking on expensive shag carpeting.

Incidentally, two of my most awful experiences as a professional writer have involved famous quarterbacks and their less famous evangelical fathers. In retrospect, God's good and sovereign hand was evident in both situations. Oddly, last night's experience gave me a strange sympathy for both men, and by the grace of God, the wounds from those experiences are long healed and mostly forgotten. But I felt sympathy, I guess, because of the visibility of their son's position and the accompanying stress, and because of the fact that whenever their sons fumble a snap or throw a ball into the dirt, everybody is looking at them.

My son did fine. He and his teammates played and fought valiantly, in spite of some very dubious officiating (two "defensive holding" calls on successive running plays—really?) and also some dubious play calling (see: three-play playbook). It was, all things considered, a beautiful night of football, but being that it's junior high football, after the loss the kids were required to act as though they'd just had a family member die. No smiling, laughing, or talking on the bus ride home, even though they're kids who just played an amazing game and have their whole lives in front of them to be glum, quiet, surly, and disappointed about a litany of things way more important than this. This enforced glumness is a football tradition that I hate.

On my way out I caught the eye of the eighth-grade quarterback's father. His son played a brave and sensational game—but lost by two points. He spent the entire evening standing alone at the edge of the bleachers. "Which one is your son?" I asked.

"Number seven, the quarterback," he replied.

"He's a heckuva player. Played a heckuva brave game tonight," I said.

And then he looked me in the eye and said, "Thank you, sir. Thank you so much. That means a lot."

And that is why I love football.

13

THE SOLDIER

Nate Boyer

When I query snapping coach Gary Zauner about his client Nate Boyer, he responds almost immediately with Boyer's videos and a large photo taken of the player as a part of Zauner's camp package. The photo shows a beefed-up Boyer (he snapped at a relatively light 195 at Texas) smiling for the camera, and I'm struck by the fact that I'm looking at a man with a semi-ruddy tan, crow's feet around his eyes, semi-bloated physique (being that he was trying to beef up to the requisite 230), and lots of backstory. There is something almost indicting in Boyer's image: the reminder that I'm too old to be doing this.

Boyer snapped well enough at Zauner's camp and then in college, to secure an invitation to Seattle Seahawks camp, where he was paired with another unconventional NFL story: head coach Pete Carroll.

"The NFL was way less nerve-racking than college," Boyer explains. "It was just fun. . . . I had a blast . . . which is probably mostly a product of the way Pete [Carroll] does things." Boyer's voice and diction are part Midwest, part bro-boy hard-ass, and part West Coast chill. The most significant part, maybe, is the age and experience. Talking to Boyer is like talking to a peer in that we've both lived some life.

When I catch up with him on the phone he's fresh off his training-camp cut and in Hollywood, taking a series of meetings with agents, book people, and others who are, ostensibly, about the business of bringing his epic life to the bookshelf or screen. But he's quick to provide context to the camp cut. "All but one of the snappers in this year's class were cut on the same day," he explains. "And the guy from the Patriots [Joe Cardona, of Navy] who had a rough preseason only made it because he was such a high investment [a fifth-round draft choice]."

What Boyer is explaining is the uniqueness of the job market—the fact that in a given year there may only be one actual instance of job turnover in his field. This year, a handful of great college snappers all received the call from the "Turk," visited the coach, and brought their playbooks. They all packed garbage bags with the contents of their lockers and flew home, disappointed, on the same day. As such, he realizes his clock is ticking, and while he's keeping his options open and fielding occasional calls from teams, he is also working on other things, such as resuming a film dream left over from adolescence.

"It's not like I'm waiting by the phone at all," he says. "I'm getting lots of opportunities and I'm saying yes to all of them. It's crazy, I spoke at a Microsoft corporate event last week. They told the skeleton of my story, but I filled in a lot of the details."

I imagine the burly and slightly out-of-place Boyer being escorted into the sleek, modern Microsoft facility and telling the story of an epic, but odd, life to a roomful of guys who have watched a lot of action movies but have probably experienced very little of it themselves. They are, like all of us, looking for a hit of inspiration in otherwise drab and predictable lives. Boyer's story provides that hit and reminds us that, just maybe, "anything is possible" could be more than an empty graduation-address platitude.

Regarding the Epic Life, Boyer says, "People are usually worried about what other people will think. They don't realize what's possible."

Boyer graduated from high school in 1999, a year in which most current NFL rookies were just learning to ride a bike and starting first grade. In 1999, Boyer, like many testosterone-laden American white boys, was being swept off his feet by David Fincher's *Fight Club* in that the movie pretty heavy-handedly captured a lot of the angst (corporations are bad) and charm (bonding is good) that goes along with being young and male. We conspicuously avoid pointing out that the film doesn't hold up when viewed as an adult, but that's immaterial. What matters is that it mattered to us then.

Inspired in part by the film, Boyer moved to Hollywood and tried to make it as an actor. As an actor his job would have been, largely, the portrayal of the epic lives of others. He's thirty-four years old now, and after some relief work in Darfur, decided he wanted to become a soldier. Boyer became a Green Beret—a Herculean effort that breaks most tough men—and served multiple tours in both Iraq and Afghanistan. "My mom rolled her eyes when I told her I wanted to be a Green Beret," he recalls.

"It was some of the most grueling training imaginable," Boyer told an NFL Films interviewer. "But I wanted to go and fight for people who couldn't defend themselves." Ultimately, in a class of 157 elite Green Beret recruits, he was one of only eleven to make it.

"I guess it was just something that tugged at me," Boyer told NFL Films, of his football dream. "It was just a regret I had that I didn't play."

Boyer received a Bronze Star for his service in the U.S. Army Special Forces. Afterward, he walked into the no doubt palatial office of then Texas coach Mack Brown and asked for a chance to try out for the football team at one of the biggest and most storied programs in America. Brown agreed, thinking that he was signing an inspirational feel-good story and a bit of locker-room maturity. At first, Boyer was a scout-team safety and got to run the flag out of the tunnel on game days.

"Initially he thought I'd just be a great asset to the locker room," says Boyer. "I'm not much of a rah-rah guy . . . but hopefully they noticed how hard I worked. I enjoyed going hard and trying to compete with those guys." By "those guys" he means the best that America has to offer in terms of high school football talent—guys who were UnderArmour All-Americans and in ESPN's Top 100. Boyer, by contrast, was a little guy who had never played a down of high school football.

"I think what the military taught me was a lot of self-confidence, self-efficacy, and self-belief," he says. "I believe that I can literally do anything with anybody, and alongside anybody."

Boyer went to that great postmodern repository of information in his quest to become a college football player. He taught himself to snap by watching YouTube videos overseas between his freshman and sophomore seasons, which is a rather significant middle finger in the direction of those who insist on thousands of hours and dollars spent on camps and travel. By repetition, and constant tweaking, Boyer settled on a snapping stroke that allowed him to log over five hundred successful snaps at Texas.

He tells the story of his first ever in-game long snap against New Mexico State, in a game that Texas was winning handily. I ask him where the nerves were worse, in a football game or a foxhole. He went on to serve as the Longhorns' primary snapper on punts and field goals for three seasons, during which he was named a three-time first-team Academic All Big-12 selection. He was also named the 2012–2013 Big-12 Sportsperson of the Year.

"I never really got it (nerves) from football," he says. "It's just a game. Nobody's dying. I think the fans are way too into it . . . living and dying by what happens on the field. Going into combat is different. All you're worried about is the man next to you once the bullets start flying."

＊ ＊ ＊

I am a lifelong football addict, and like all addicts I like my fixes to come in a particular way. I've played and coached the sport my entire life and, as such, I have an almost physical ache for it each fall. Ideally I'm playing it, but in lieu of that I'm at least watching a lot, ideally in person.

When I learned that I'd be teaching at a football-less university in Jackson, Tennessee, I immediately started scoping out the college football in the area and found that there isn't much. The University of Tennessee at Knoxville is six hours away. Memphis is an hour, and tickets are expensive. But then I learned that there is a college with football—Lane College—right in my city, and very nearly in my backyard.

My first weekend here I drove through Lane's campus and found it fascinating: old, stately buildings in an older part of town. I drove by their practice field and was disappointed that there were no players on it. I wanted to watch a practice and just be near it (like I said, a sickness). Lane is an HBCU (stands for Historically Black Colleges and Universities) and has an interesting history with my school. When a couple of my best journalism students said, "We should start a journalism partnership with Lane," I enthusiastically agreed—for reasons both philosophical and, admittedly, selfish. Lane has something that I want, and that something is college football. A civil-rights hero I am not.

The partnership has been everything that I'd hoped it would be: fun, stimulating, enriching, and redemptive for students and faculty on both sides. It's early, and nothing is ever perfect, but I'm hopeful. Today was Lane's first home football game. They play on a retro high school field here in Jackson whose defining characteristic is a set of very crooked goalposts. The stands are brick, and old. Paint peels. Grass yellows in the bright sun. Rap music throbs out of portable speakers but soon gives way to drumlines and the best marching-band music I have ever heard in my entire life.

On my way in, a Lane College professor greeted me with a warm hug. Another offered me barbecue, on the house. I met Lane's president, who was warm and hospitable. The game opened with a very evangelical prayer in which both teams, both bands, and both sets of fans bowed heads and prayed for goodwill and harmony between the schools. In all my years of football I've never seen anything like it. My son Maxim and I sat on the front row, just a few feet away from the Lane bench. And though the game was hard and violent—as all good football games are hard and violent—it had zero fights and almost no profanity. At no point did I have to cover my son's ears, as I've had to do so many times at Spartan Stadium, Ford Field, and many of the other venues we've frequented over the years, where buffoonery is the norm.

Today we played Tuskeegee, and their white jerseys were emblazoned with the word "Skeegee" (note: I'm an avid jersey collector and want one—bad). Their players, like ours, danced to the marching-band music during warm-ups. Swagger was present in droves, but it was an unselfconscious kind of redemptive swag. I stood along a fence and noticed a young boy, about my son's age, with his eyes closed and head swaying, dancing (as they say) as if nobody was watching. A lone Tuskeegee player knelt and prayed in the end zone before the game.

The football wasn't perfect—far from it, in fact. There were, I think, six turnovers in the first nine minutes. Both teams ran the spread offense (no fullbacks, lots of bubble screens), which I hate. Lane lost 40–14, but it didn't matter. It was a beautiful day of live college football with a team I'm now calling my own. I will be back the very next time they play at home and each time thereafter. Both bands played back and forth at one another, battle style, the entire afternoon. "I could listen to this music all day long," I told my son.

He looked at me like I was crazy and started climbing the fence as if he owned the place and as if there was never even a moment of weirdness or division between black and white in Jackson, Tennessee.

✿ ✿ ✿

I'm not sure when I realized that my arena team for spring, the Pineywoods Bucks, had folded. I teach at Union University, and one of my students, who was doing a writing project for the Bucks, approached me saying, "Kluck, they haven't posted on Facebook in a month, and their website is down. Also, the owner won't return any calls or e-mails."

Ouch. I played it cool but then immediately sent my own unreturned calls and e-mails into the ether. "Michael, this is Ted Kluck with the snapping book project . . . just checking in!" Trying to keep it light and cheerful, when what I really wanted to say was, "Michael, I can't help but notice that it looks like our team has folded. What's going on?"

The message, sadly, was clear: I need to begin looking for another team in order to snap one more time, put the demons to rest, and finish this book. In my mind I'm vacillating between the one-off Plimpton-style "Isn't it quirky to have a writer on board" angle and an angle wherein I *really* play for a *real* team because I can actually snap well and actually belong there. This angle, obviously, has appeal—in part because I am snapping really well now, in that I'm snapping pretty consistently into targets but am almost perfect when I get to snap to real people.

That reality has made me consider (gulp) semi-pro again, an experience that has been historically a very mixed bag in that on the low end it has put me in the hospital (broken collarbone) and once ended with a gun-and-knife fight at halftime of a game. It goes without saying that I didn't wield a gun or a knife, but just the proximity was disconcerting. I have "retired" many times, only to find my way back onto websites and onto eBay to buy equipment because there is something very sickly comforting about all of it, and something flattering about being "needed" by a team—even a pathetic and disorganized mess of one in the middle of nowhere. This is all an elaborate way of saying that I've been surfing a lot of semi-pro team websites lately.

My friend Jon Akemon is dealing with the ebb and flow of his dream as well. He has flown north to a small town in New York, where he is a member of the Hudson Valley Fort, in year two of the Fall Experimental Football League (FXFL). FXFL commissioner Brian Woods, according to financial reports on the league, may be in over his head and in the unenviable but understandable position of having purchased something really cool that he can no longer afford. But in his case it's a pro football league, and his labor force is comprised of big, angry people who want the money that's been promised to them.

Jon has agonized over whether to report to Hudson Valley at all, and we have had many late-night conversations about it—the kinds in which I try to put myself in the position of a wise older brother or father figure. The fact of the matter is that Jon is unsure whether to go and put himself in harm's way for little to no money. It's not an easy choice. But there's a contract with his name on it, and a helmet in a locker with his name on it. This is seductive.

He decides to report, and shortly thereafter his coach—former Houston Cougars legend John Jenkins—leaves mysteriously before the first game. There are rumors that no one in the league is being paid. The FXFL season opener takes place in a monsoon at a Coney Island minor league ballpark and features former NFL first round draft choice Josh Freeman, a quarterback who washed out of the NFL due to a combination of poor play and (apparent) character issues. My prevailing thought while watching an Internet stream of the game (Brooklyn Bolts versus Florida Blacktips) is that everyone looks as if they're freezing and they'd rather be anywhere else doing anything else.

The stands are empty, and the football is awful because of the weather. Freeman turns the ball over a ton, and I think Brooklyn loses, but I'm not sure because I really don't care. I decide that in the sports entertainment business, context and presentation are everything. A few short years ago, Freeman looked like a Greek god, being that he played in the NFL in a fresh and form-fitting Nike uniform each week, with 150 camera angles, in high-definition, in a full-stadium that was produced to the hilt. Here, on a minor league field in a baggy jersey in a monsoon with one camera angle, he looks like an ordinary person and it makes me sad.

Jon is marooned in upstate New York at a c-list motel with forty-five other dissatisfied football exiles. It's a recipe for disaster. He suits up for the first game and snaps without incident. The game was supposed to be streamed on ESPN3 but wasn't. Each day I wonder if he will send the text saying, "I'm done. I got what I came for." At the end of the day, he's not there for money as much as he's there for film—film being the mysterious, ethereal conduit to scouts, who are themselves somewhat mysterious conduits to teams. He's there because he needs current snapping film. Mission accomplished.

"Even without a formal partnership, the FXFL has already cultivated a symbiotic relationship with its bigger brother in its first two years," reported the *Wall Street Journal.*

> Around 95% of its players arrived for the season in September after being cut from NFL training-camp rosters. Since the FXFL season ends in November, after the NFL's trade deadline, players have the chance to catch on with an injury-ravaged NFL roster. And unlike in the Canadian Football League, where players sign one-year deals with a team option for a second season, FXFL players are free to leave for the NFL whenever they want.

Despite the FXFL's tenuous financial footing, Akemon texts photographs of his helmet and stadium—such is the conflicted life of the football player.

Weeks in the fall, at present, are marked by an almost constant but never-really-satisfying barrage of football. The NFL has decided that it needs to play on Sunday, Monday, and also Thursday. ESPN long ago decided that it was profitable and right to showcase such juggernauts as Middle Tennessee State and Bowling Green on Tuesday and Thursday nights. That said, there's a lot of football to watch, but the sort of aggregate of all of it means that none of it is that exciting. It all seems, this season, to just be an excuse to promote "one-week fantasy football."

I used to occasionally cover fights in Las Vegas and, as such, got a ringside seat (as it were, pun intended) to what real, deep-seated, and chronic self-loathing looked like, being that Las Vegas was (and is) the self-loathing capital of the free world. Simply stated, Vegas is an easy place to ruin your life in a variety of ways.

So it was that in the middle of about the eighty-fourth straight hour of advertising for "one-week fantasy football! get paid immediately!" I realized what I was seeing in ad after miserable ad: the Las Vegas male. Both companies—FanDuel and DraftKings—offer legalized sports gambling in America, which you used to have to go to a sportsbook in a Las Vegas casino to do. Now it's available to anyone with a computer, and this is why roughly an hour of every three-hour NFL telecast seems to be dedicated to ads for both companies.

The ads are the same in that they include a guy speaking who is supposed to look "regular" in that his face is a little shiny, a little bloated, and a little bit like yours. He's wearing a hoody or a T-shirt. He is twenty-eight, thirty-two, twenty-six, or thirty-five years old. He is the age you are. That's the point. He probably, like you, spends his professional life glued to a computer and then, according to the ad, spends his free time glued to a different computer "just picking his players and getting paid immediately!" He has a slightly predatory look in his bulbous eye as if he were in Vegas for his buddy's bachelor party and, you know, if things went well he'd probably try to sleep with your cousin, sister, or daughter and then go back to his suite and guffaw about it with his other friends who are also just picking their players and making money.

He's super clever and so are his friends.

What's disconcerting is that the youngish, dirtbag American male no longer has an obvious "look" inasmuch as he no longer has tattoos, long hair, or some obvious "tell"—the likes of which your mother used to tell you to avoid. The new self-loathing American male probably went to college and has a decent job. What's interesting is that they obviously and intentionally didn't use attractive or charismatic people in these ads; rather, they cast the guy next door (subtext: your next-door neighbor is just picking his players and getting paid immediately, so why aren't you?).

Other images in the ads are as follows: guys having fun in bars; high fiving; a giant cardboard check; male guffawing; money wafting down from the heavens; and more male guffawing.

There's something Pavlovian and also just plain relentless about these companies and ads. They're on literally all the time during any sort of male-oriented television or radio programing. They're just waiting for you to relent and enter the discount code. They know that you will, eventually. They know that you'll be back next week because you want the games to "Mean Something" and you think that putting a little money on these players will render meaningless games meaningful.

What they're promising is, of course, "action." And the role that action plays is that it promises to make otherwise boring lives a little less boring. Except that in pursuing the "action" (substitute booze, drugs, cheap sex, pornography, etc., here), the pursuer always wakes up feeling a little bit less satisfied and looking a little bit more hollowed out, Vegasy, and sad in the same fashion as the guys in these ads. Somehow, you know it isn't going to go well for the guys in these ads. You intuit that they're probably mediocre at their jobs and their wives probably hate them for extremely legitimate reasons. Even though it is raining cash on their heads, in the ads, something inside reminds you that you're looking at a loser.

You may be asking, "What makes you any different, Kluck?" And my answer is absolutely nothing. I have known just enough of potentially life-ruining, Vegas-style idiocy that these ads are actually terrifying to me. Looking at the guys in these ads is like looking in the mirror at an unredeemed, un-Christlike, bitter, and hopeless version of myself. It's chilling.

There's nothing as sleepless and dissatisfied as a Las Vegas morning. The only answer to it is to take a hot shower and get on an airplane as quickly as possible, so you shuffle into the airport and find your gate, walking past other miserable-looking guys exactly your age wearing your super-unique T-shirt and your facial hair who are miserable for exactly the same reasons—because the action they so desired left them feeling dissatisfied and guilty.

So this is the aggregate effect of watching a lot of football this fall—now with the presence of one-week fantasy football. It may be my age, but the glittering dream of the NFL glitters a little bit less. It's looking more and more like just a high-paying, short-lived, very risky job.

* * *

After leaving the Fort (heh), Akemon calls me from Kansas City, where he is in town to take in the Steelers/Chiefs game.

There is nothing like an NFL game in an NFL stadium to cause grown men to dream. Jon is experiencing Big Context—in that the game seems a little more immortal when it's in front of you in all its big-money Technicolor glory. The players look a little bigger. The fans look a little more worshipful. Every hip-hop song and every big-screen replay is meant to elicit a very specific reaction. It all looks as if it's perfect and will never go away. When you're in the midst of Big Context, you feel like you need it forever.

The father in me wants very badly to talk him down off this imaginary high that he's on. The fact of the matter is that he *can* be down on that field. He's been close, recently, in the Titans minicamp and on the FXFL field, and if things had broken differently, he'd be there. But in a way it must be torturous for him to be there in the stadium but not really Be There.

But I've felt this many times and in fact still feel it every time I go to an NFL game. Football seems like a good idea when you see it in this context, so instead of talking Akemon down off his artificial ledge, I instead give him the number for an agent friend of mine.

"He has guys in the league, and he works hard and has a ton of integrity," I say. These are knowable things about my agent friend. But I can't promise a workout with a team. Nobody can. It's tough in this role with Jon, in that I don't know if I should be the encouraging buddy or the parental voice of reason. I was an only child, and I think, as such, my parents sort of bought into the idea that I was special for a while, if only because they had no one else in the house to which to compare me. I was, in fact, wholly average: an average athlete, an average student, average looking, and moderately funny—average.

For a while they were dream encouragers, but then there came a time, in my early twenties, when their perspective shifted drastically to that of the dream-dashing wet blanket. I resented them for it for a while, but I know that they were doing it out of love. They wanted to make sure that I crucified my NFL dream so that I didn't spend the rest of my life hating where I was. This is the double-edged nature of dreams. It can be really fun to have something to dream about, but having something to dream about can really make the rest of your life seem crappy by comparison. I sense this tension in Jon.

I'm not at all surprised when I learn that the FXFL has limped to the finish line, cancelling a Hudson Valley game and apparently not paying players in the league "title" game. It's a sad story, and yet the latest in the long litany of alternate-football-league-related failures. I think this can be attributed to what is commonly called "Mission Drift." At one level, the stated mission of the FXFL was to be a "developmental" league—that is, a place where NFL-hopeful players could practice, compete, stay sharp, and get film for their agents. On this level, the league "worked" in the sense that games were played and film was made. Where the league failed was on every other level, including

- building a meaningful fan base;
- making a meaningful TV ripple;
- paying players;
- putting a professional-looking product on the field (including but not limited to everything from camera angles to uniforms and gameday pomp and circumstance); and
- avoiding lawsuits.

My thought is, what if you just removed everything in the aforementioned list from the equation? My idea is as follows:

1. Create a true developmental league (and by league I mean a centrally housed collective that could be as small as *one* team but could grow indefinitely).
2. Embed the league, from a management standpoint, inside the sports management program at a university of any size, provided that the university has at least one practice field indoors and outdoors. That being the case, day-to-day administrative tasks could be filled by student interns for college credit and players could be housed in unused campus dormitories during breaks in the academic calendar. There could be a "summer season" and a "winter season" during each major break. "Seasons" could be as short as two to three weeks.
3. Remove the burden of fans entirely—meaning no stadium rental, no concessions workforce, no parking, no marketing, no promotion, and no travel. This also removes the burden of sales.
4. Play "games" in ideal conditions, only for the purposes of securing film. From a football standpoint, game scenarios can be requested by subscribing NFL teams (more below), meaning that if a team wants to see two-minute drills, a "game" can deliver multiple examples. Ditto for short yardage, inside run, and so forth.
5. Don't pay players a penny but offer insurance. Pay elite coaches. Players and their agents will opt in because it's a competitive environment and a chance for film. It goes without saying, but it's an opportunity for unemployed coaches to stay sharp/competitive as well.
6. Profit is generated in two primary ways: (a) agents will pay fees to secure positions for their players, not unlike the way that fees are

paid for precombine and predraft training/instruction; and (b) NFL and CFL teams will pay subscription fees for in-person access to the practice sessions and games and for delivery of practice and game films.

It's really never been realistic to think that a relatively cash-poor minor league could generate enough of a fan base or TV presence to become a profitable sports-entertainment product. My scenario just removes the "entertainment" piece entirely, leaving the possibility for growth if the model takes off. Players still get the opportunity to hone skills in a competitive environment, and subscribing NFL teams have an unprecedented level of "control" over the whole process, which they'll like.

14

SILVERDOME AND THE ONWARD MARCH OF TIME

Out of the crash site of what's left of the Fall Experimental Football League (FXFL) has emerged my next move, from a football standpoint. Jon Akemon has put me in touch with a guy named Zen Bliss who coaches an AIFL (American Indoor Football League) team called Mile High Menace. Bliss—currently the running backs coach at Allegheny College in Pennsylvania—is a football vagabond; he is a mercenary coach for hire who has coached indoor, semi-pro, high school, and college ball. Basically, like me, he's an addict. Our drugs are new football experiences.

"I called in a favor, and he's going to let you play," Jon explains. I exhale for now, but like all things in the world of semi-pro and indoor ball, I'll believe it when I'm suiting up and jogging out for warm-ups. Until that moment, it can all go away.

What's also weird is keeping my thirty-nine-year-old body and snapping stroke functional and tuned up before then. My elbows and knees are hurting now. Maybe I'm snapping and lifting too much? And I've developed a weird little hitch at the beginning of my snapping stroke. It is unacceptable but is happening on some weird, psychological, neurotic, "can't really help it" level. On the plus side, I'm stronger than I've been in years. Benching 225 pounds for reps feels easy. My upper body is thick and muscular, and it is the tenuous dream of suiting up again (see above, re: the double-edged nature of this) that is fueling these workouts. I flip tractor tires in the early morning fieldhouse chill. I see the other old faculty guys in the gym, reading their academic journals and wearing their weird workout clothes, and I feel smugly superior because I'm gonna be in a football uniform in a few months.

But how dumb is it that while I'm in the midst of a dream job—teaching writing on a gorgeous college campus in the South, where the sun is forever shining—I'm still dreaming of the helmet and the turf? There is something seriously wrong with me.

"I'm sorry I've been such a bitch about football lately," my wife confesses, in the car. She has been, but still, it's incredibly sweet and gracious of her to admit it. It got weird the other day when we were discussing school options for my thirteen-year-old. I mentioned his football as a factor in the decision, and she flipped out, asserting that it "shouldn't really be a factor." Awkward silence ensued. It's cool of her to apologize, and this will be a lifelong conversation, made more complicated by every new media release about another punch-drunk former football player struggling with postconcussion symptoms. This is legitimately scary, but (in all honesty) probably not scary enough to keep me off the field.

I know this: my wife loves me, and she loves my son. She doesn't want to see us eternally screwed up by this stupidly addictive game.

Another interesting development has been the Silverdome film project, manned now by a collection of people—Glenn Pakulak, Nate Boyer, the sports agent Eugene Lee, and Akemon—I've collected during the course of this book's development. I wrote a film about a fictional USFL quarterback who leaves his stable, suburban home and life to go and live as a squatter in the falling-down Pontiac Silverdome—the only place he ever felt whole.

"You collect people," my wife explains. And by "people" she usually means young men who are dreamers and who need something they feel I can provide—and usually that "something" is encouragement to pursue a dream of some kind. In this case it's the shared dream of making Silverdome before the very looming deadline of the city of Pontiac deciding to bulldoze the eyesore.

                     o o o

Michigan State University has always had a bit of an inferiority complex. Famously called "the younger brother" by the University of Michigan's star tailback Mike Hart, one of America's oldest and largest land-grant universities is sadly better known for its rioting (postwin *and* postloss—the outcome doesn't seem to matter) and its basketball titles, collected under coach Tom Izzo.

I lived in the East Lansing area for over a decade, and my memories of the place include a pervasive and almost permanent gloom—cloud cover, sleet, and eventually snow—that descends over the area in November and stays until April or May. That said, almost every Spartan game I ever attended took place in either cold or wet conditions. Spartan Stadium is a giant, old concrete bowl with metal bleachers in which the "seats" are about six inches wide. Fans tailgate in campus parking lots and (famously) on some tennis courts adjacent to the stadium. This is always where the bulk of the real tailgating takes place.

Ann Arbor, Michigan, by contrast, has an air of upscale liberality. It's like a giant Starbucks. It's a great place to wax smug and superior about "materialism" while at the same time getting fully outfitted for your next ski trip. Ann Arbor is wineries and boutiques, whereas East Lansing is shot-and-beer bars for the hourly workers at whatever GM plants haven't closed yet, and the khaki drones and name badges who have the really coveted jobs in state government.

In Ann Arbor, the best tailgating happens on a golf course, which is somehow fitting. Tonight, Michigan State is in town for the annual renewal of a bitter and brutal rivalry that means more this year because both teams matter. After a long run of Michigan dominance, the tables turned for a number of years as Michigan ground through a few bad-fit coaches such as Rich Rodriguez (the spread offense in Ann Arbor—gah! And he's not a "Michigan Man"! Gah again!) and Brady Hoke (great guy, bad coach). Michigan State has been led by the always miserable-looking Mark Dantonio, who has enjoyed (or not enjoyed, as it were) an unprecedented level of success that has included Big Ten Championships and Rose Bowl appearances.

Michigan's journey out of the desert of mediocrity is helmed by former star quarterback Jim Harbaugh, he of the almost cartoonishly lantern jaw and famous intensity. Harbaugh is what a little kid would draw if you gave him a pencil and said "Draw a hero quarterback." Harbaugh had a long, successful run as an NFL quarterback before turning around the program at another upscale, brainy school (Stanford). He then went to San Francisco, where he took the 49ers to a

Super Bowl that he lost to his brother, John, and his Baltimore Ravens. Harbaugh's famous intensity was thought to be a little much for the typical NFL player, so he negotiated a Returning Hero narrative with Michigan, which narrative he ushered in by (no joke) pulling a lady out of a burning car on Interstate 96.

Thus far the Wolverines are a surprising one-loss team populated largely with the same players who were unsuccessful the year before. They will beat Michigan State in this game by doing what Michigan State typically does: lining up with multiple tight ends and a fullback and battering the life out of their opponent with a big tailback, in this case the mini-dreadlocked Deveon Smith who at five foot ten and 225 looks as if he was made to carry the ball in a Jim Harbaugh smash-mouth offense. Quarterback Jake Rudock is tasked primarily with handing the ball off and throwing short to talented tight end Jake Butt. He does so for the majority of the game. Rudock is a fifth-year senior, fresh off a transfer from Iowa, where he started for two seasons. This mercenary graduate year is a reality of modern college football, and it's strange to see a player at one school suiting up for a rival school the next season.

Michigan State's quarterback is Connor Cook, who has been hyped as a potential first-round NFL draft choice. He is universally accepted as a Great Player, except that he doesn't really play that great. If he were a color he'd be beige. Even though he is a returning senior quarterback, and a projected first-round pick, his teammates didn't elect him a team captain. This is a subnarrative that will follow Cook through the draft process.

Michigan State's first series ends in a punt, and snapper Taybor Pepper's first snap is low. Pepper, like Michigan's snapper (more below), is a veteran of many Chris Rubio camps and has the Rubio publicity machine largely to thank for his scholarship at Michigan State (along with his talent and hard work). Both schools feature snappers who are on full scholarships.

Both players will be snapping off FieldTurf at the Big House, which is heavenly because it involves none of the irregularities (mud, clumps of grass, long grass, short grass, etc.) that come with natural turf. My wife makes the observation that Michigan State's all-white road uniforms, with white cleats, look oddly pajama-like. I don't disagree. Pepper's next punt snap is a laser, right at the chest of the punter.

Michigan snapper Scott Sypniewski is a little high on his first snap, but the punter boots an eighty-yarder that trickles down inside the MSU five-yard line. The crowd goes wild, and for the moment, the punter is a hero. His name is unimportant at the moment because, as long as punters are doing their jobs, we rarely notice them.

The teams batter each other with inside runs. It's cold. Network talking head and former legendary tough guy Chris Spielman uses the phrase "Old School Football" several times. There is a great moment in the second quarter in which, after Michigan linebacker Joe Bolden is ejected from the game after a questionable "targeting" call, he runs the perimeter of the field, waving his arms and firing up the home crowd. He is Michigan's leading tackler. The targeting penalty is an attempt to make safer a game that is, by definition, unsafe. There have been legitimate instances of this, but Bolden got screwed. He whips the crowd into a crazed froth.

Pepper is low with another snap, late in the second quarter. Regarding joyless intensity and paranoia, neither head coach opens their practice sessions to the media. Michigan State apparently opens practice for ten minutes on Thursdays, which is almost more of an insult to the media than an olive branch. With 1:16 remaining in the first half, Michigan punter Blake O'Neill has to field a snap off his shoe tops in order to get a punt away. It is a harbinger of things to come.

The game will come down to what should be a routine punt snap from a previously anonymous snapper named Sypniewski. It's a good Michigan name: Polish and with strong old-timey football connotations. His dad was a center at Michigan and may have the attendant lifetime of pain and injuries to show for it. Snapping, by comparison, seems like a relatively safe way to continue the family legacy and continue suiting up for the good old maize and blue, cognizant of the fact that things that happen in this game become part of highlight packages that will exist and be viewed until the end of mankind (or at least for another decade until football is outlawed completely).

With ten seconds remaining Michigan leads 23–21 and is in full run-out-the-clock mode; however, their series comes to an end, and they need to punt the ball away. Sypniewski, wearing number 31, jogs onto the artificial turf and bends over the ball, as he has done thousands of times before. There are photos online of a beaming Sypniewski signing his letter of intent, surrounded by a throng of officially licensed Family

Members. There's a photo of the kid, still beaming, faxing the letter to the Michigan football offices. Everything that happens in today's football economy happens for an audience. Everything is made for television (and by that I mean made for the Internet).

Also made for television (literally, in this case) are the shots of Michigan's maize-shirted crowd, buzzing with anticipation—thousands of affluent, North-Facey kids anticipating the awesome party that is to follow this signature win.

There are photos online of Sypniewski standing shoulder to shoulder with Michigan State snapper Taybor Pepper when both were apple-cheeked high school recruits. They look like children. Now they are snapping on national television and in front of a hundred thousand plus in the Big House.

"When I say someone is a five-star snapper, Scott is," Rubio told the *Detroit Free Press* in 2013 when the snapper was signed. He indicated that he had worked with Sypniewski over thirty times. "He's someone you don't have to worry about, like a Honda Accord. The car starts every time and gives no problems. With Sypniewski, you expect this is the only interview about him, and he'll be there four years."

"No. 1, his (snapping) speed is very, very good, 0.7 (seconds)," continued Rubio in the same piece. "From there, the accuracy, when you launch 15 yards away (the kicker/punter) should have to move. Obviously his thickness and athletic ability is good. The big one is mentality—how can he handle himself? A long snapper misses a snap, and he's got to sit there 40 minutes waiting for another chance. Mentally, you have to be strong, and he is."

And Rubio's laudatory presigning scouting report reads,

> Sypniewski is just flat out fantastic! Ball is like a missle [sic] yet very easy to catch. Movement is flawless and he is snapping with ease. Looks like he is not even trying but, before you blink, the ball is right on your hip. Accuracy, consistency and speed are all excellent. A tad lighter on his feet could bump him up and I am being picky. Sypniewski is terrific and is snapping with a *ton* of confidence. I am fully expecting him to stick his chest out and dominate in Vegas.

Sypniewski bends over the ball. The win will be a signature one in the already-impressive Harbaugh oeuvre—to knock off one of the legitimate Big Boys on the Big Ten block in his first season.

Michigan's punter is a handsome kid from Australia named Blake O'Neill. He will shoulder almost all the blame for what is about to transpire. O'Neill comes to the Wolverines via Weber State (Big Sky Conference) and Australian Rules Football (where he suffered "a split liver") before that. He, like Rudock, is a graduate student enjoying the mercenary fifth-year option. He did some runway modeling in Australia to put himself through undergraduate school. The world, it seems, is his oyster. Oh, to be young, handsome, working on your master's, doing some modeling, and punting for the University of Michigan. Life could be worse.

But regarding what actually transpires: Sypniewski, cognizant of the fact that a high snap would be disastrous, probably takes something off the snap. The result is a ball that seems to die in the air—like a sinker— about a yard and a half before it gets to O'Neill. The punter has to sort of awkwardly step toward it, and the snap hits his hands at about shin level. O'Neill then, horrifically, drops the football. It is picked up by a backup Michigan State defensive back who runs it into the end zone for the victory, which is celebrated upon so vigorously that he breaks a hip while lying on the turf with the football. Cut to shocked-looking North Face kids, sad faces. Cut to celebrating Michigan State Spartans whose run of Big Ten Conference luck, dating back to Kirk Cousins's Hail Mary a few years ago, is astonishing. Harbaugh looks as if he wants to kill someone.

O'Neill takes the fall. He receives the now-obligatory, now-cliché death threats on Twitter. He endures the tacky O'Neill-related Halloween costumes, appearing the following week. His postgame comments evidence a surprising (and nearly offensive) amount of perspective. "Pick yourself up, dust yourself off, and go again," he told the *Detroit Free Press*. "That's the beauty of sport. You get a chance to prove yourself again against Minnesota."

Doesn't he realize how *important* this all is?

Sypniewski will continue to struggle. A few weeks later, the Wolverines travel to Bloomington, Indiana, to take on the perennially bottom-dwelling Indiana Hoosiers. The beauty of sports is that, as O'Neill said, there is a new battle to fight each week, a new venue, another plane ride, another luxury hotel, and another game program sitting on the stool in your locker. And thankfully there are games on the schedule such as the Indiana game, which have annually provided program's such as Michigan's with the opportunity to "get healthy" with an easy win.

These Michigan-at-Indiana telecasts usually unfold as follows: camera shots of the lovely fall colors in Bloomington, followed by Indiana University keeping it respectable for a half, and then proceeding to get blown out by a much stronger, deeper Michigan squad. Finally, after nearly two decades' worth of sartorial wandering, the Indiana uniform has settled back where it needs to be: the block, cream-colored "I" sitting on a simple background of crimson. It figured to be the most hopeful thing about the Hoosiers.

But this year they deviate from the script. Indiana's two best offensive players, six-foot-six pocket quarterback Nate Sudfeld and slashing running back Jordan Howard, are arguably more talented than anyone on Michigan's offense. Howard carries the ball thirty-five times for 238 yards and two scores and Sudfeld is good enough to keep the chains occasionally moving through the air. Against all reason, Indiana remains "in" the game late into the second half, where things once again get weird for Sypniewski and Michigan's kick teams.

Specifically, he bounces a field-goal snap to the holder, resulting in a third-quarter miss, and then misses wide and low later, a snap that punter Blake O'Neill is able to masterfully redeem. It is a stroke of poetic justice. What Sypniewski is experiencing is a terrifying sense of the body knowing how to do an activity it has done thousands of times but the mind playing ghastly tricks.

As the telecast cuts to commercial before the overtime period, another snapper is seen warming up on the Michigan sideline. How this will all end for Sypniewski has become the driving narrative, for me. I may be witnessing the end of a snapping career and, aside from his parents, may be the only one who notices.

But then something crazy happens. Michigan will be required to score twice to beat Indiana in a scrappy overtime period (and will do so), and after each score, Sypniewski will drill home a perfect extra-point snap. He has stayed in the game and, for now, has overcome the mental anguish that caused him to roll back his earlier snaps. I'm mightily impressed. For at least another week, he still exists.

* * *

On the same Saturday, across the Midwest, the Missouri Tigers face the Brigham Young University Cougars in what would have been a semi-meaningless, midseason nonconference game but, given the magnitude of the events at Mizzou, takes on an added meaning. That is, it was essentially the protest of black football players at Mizzou that resulted in the firing of the school's president, after it was implied by student groups that he was guilty of repeated soft responses to racial issues on campus.

Head Coach Gary Pinkel and Missouri's white players supported the protest, and a day later President Tim Wolfe announced his resignation. There was also a hunger strike by a protesting student; however, it's not hard to feel as if Wolfe's resignation had a lot more to do with the horror of an SEC football team failing to show for a game (and the million-plus dollars it would lose) than the horror of a student feeling hungry.

A few days later I sit in an auditorium at my university, where we have invited students and faculty from Lane College, an HBCU (Historically Black Colleges and Universities) in town, to discuss the state of race relations on our campuses in light of the events at Missouri. The room is packed full, and it is, for the most part, a hopeful and helpful night of dialogue. What's odd, though, is that in one building over, the most visible black athletes on our predominately white campus (the acronym for this, PWI, is, I learn, a "thing"), the basketball players, are playing a meaningless nonconference tune-up game against a small-school opponent.

All student-athletes are basically on renewable one-year contracts, and as such, their work requirements are more extensive and more laden with pressure than those of a regular student selling pizzas in the evening or reshelving books at the library. The student-athletes at our PWI shuffle around, sometimes gargantuan in stature, with bags of ice Saran-wrapped to their knees. Black and white alike, they move about virtually unknown by the rest of the student population; theirs a daily schedule of morning lift, films, practice, study table, and bed. Rinse. Repeat.

The reality is that, as individuals, these athletes have no power. Athletes quit or transfer all the time, and it barely warrants a fine-print mention in a newspaper or on a school's athletic website. But the Missouri incident showed that as a collective, it is a different matter altogether. A day later the athletes mobilized, the president was looking for a new job. I've searched long and hard for a word to describe this, and the best I can do is "unsettling." As a university professor, I guess it's just scary how fast a bunch of students can get someone fired.

It occurred to me that perhaps the coolest thing that could have happened at this Lane/Union confab would have been for one or more of our black basketball players to have walked into the lecture hall, in uniform, to be a part of the event. It would have been cool if the coach had allowed them to do this, or if the team had just started the game with its white players. But none of that happened, and it's nobody's fault exactly, because what would it quantifiably have done? It would have allowed athletes to be "known" in a different way, certainly, but I think I wanted it because it would have been a grand gesture, and good or bad, as a writer, I see life in terms of grand gestures. In this regard, it's an opportunity lost.

15

WHERE'D EVERYONE GO?

The Photographer: Tyler Schmitt

The panic attacks started for long snapper Tyler Schmitt in Seattle: the elevated heart rate, the shortness of breath, the tingling in the extremities, and the feeling of black and utter hopelessness. Interesting, then, that he mentions the weather.

"I think all of the rain there, combined with my back surgery, really made it tough," he explains. Schmitt grew up in Arizona and, as such, was accustomed to sunshine. He was also accustomed to kicking ass—something his ailing body never permitted him to do in Seattle.

Actually, it's interesting that he mentions any of it at all, being that athletes and former athletes are famous for their "mental toughness." Yet Schmitt divulges all of it within the first minute of our conversation.

"I was always the best," he explains, without a hint of arrogance left. "In high school, in the Rubio camps . . . I always had the most tackles and could always snap the fastest." As a result of being one of the original Rubio devotees—there were fifteen snappers at Schmitt's first camp in Vegas—he signed with San Diego State, where people said he would never get drafted as a pure snapper. Following his successful career as an Aztec (not one bad snap there, according to his punter), he was selected in the sixth round by the Seattle Seahawks in 2008. At the time, it was the highest-ever selection for a pure snapper. Schmitt had built himself into a six-foot-two, 240-pound snapping machine.

There is the look of the classic football alpha male in Schmitt's old photos: thick neck, intimidating frown, tattoos, and huge biceps. Schmitt was what you aspired to, as a football player; he was the guy who could walk into any room and command respect.

Schmitt spans the eras—between my pre-Rubio time period and the current total suburbification of long snapping, in which the camp circuit is necessary. "You're not getting a scholarship without it," he says.

"I led the state of Arizona in sacks as a high school senior," he explains. "So it was hard for me to go to San Diego State and stand on the sidelines for two hours each practice, with everyone looking at me like a 'specialist.'" What Schmitt is describing is the delicate political balance of the football locker room, where respect must be earned. He earned it by becoming one of the strongest players on the team and making a ton of tackles.

Schmitt always preached "being an athlete," as opposed to "being a specialist." "Kids need to be more diverse," he says. "Learn all-around skills . . . train like a linebacker or defensive end. I think it's crazy that 'long-snapper' is a position you can play in Pop Warner now. I was lucky that I got a little formal training."

It is, in part, this mentality that prepared Schmitt for what he would face at San Diego State.

"I remember standing on the field playing against the University of Michigan as an eighteen-year-old freshman, just shivering with nerves," he says of the one-hundred-thousand-plus fans in the Big House. "But I kept telling myself 'this is what you're destined to do.'" The destiny narrative is a real charmer but only when it's actually working.

Rather than being the NFL dream come true, Seattle was the birthplace of isolation and depression for Schmitt. "It was the depression of, 'Wow they took a chance and drafted me in the sixth round and all of the expectations that come with that,'" he explains. "It was the guilt of letting everyone down and only lasting one season."

What's interesting to note is that you could make the argument that, to a man, all of Schmitt's 2008 draft classmates in Seattle were failures. USC pass rusher Lawrence Jackson was a bust, and ditto for second-round Notre Dame tight end John Carlson. Arguably the best player to come out of Seattle's class that year—running back Justin Forsett—has done the bulk of his best work as a Baltimore Raven. Such is the imperfect science of running an NFL draft, and the slim-chance nature of the NFL career in general.

Schmitt was felled by a back injury and subsequent operation in Seattle, and lost the entire 2008 season. Once a ripped 240 pounds, he shriveled to 205 after the surgery. Again, from experience, there is nothing more paranoia inducing for the athlete than the postsurgery shrivel in which you go from looking like a superhero to looking like the dreaded "regular person."

"They put me on IR, and I tried my hardest to put the weight back on and rehab," he says. "But I got cut."

"It was kind of a relief, initially, to be done," he explains. But Schmitt was lost, with well-meaning friends and family members encouraging him to "find a passion and pursue it!" Theirs was the American doctrine of "following your dream" being the pathway to happiness and fulfillment. "I always said, 'You think I don't want that?'" Easier said than done.

Schmitt did the only thing he knew how to do at the time and attempted a comeback, reasoning that false hope was better than no hope at all. I know this cycle well myself—the skewed logic that dreaming about something, even the wrong thing, was better than no dream at all.

"I spent about nine months training and getting back into great shape and had some tryouts lined up," he explains. But shortly before the tryout he tore a pectoral muscle in a workout, which would require yet another operation. This was followed by another six-month rehab and then a final back surgery.

Even for the most optimistic, confident, and "mentally strong" athlete, the dream can be hard to nurture, day after day, under those circumstances.

"That's when I got addicted to pain pills again," he explains. "To dull the physical pain, but also the mental pain. I was about as low as you can get."

* * *

"It was more the letdown for others," Schmitt says, of his ouster from the NFL. I understand what he's saying. Football becomes a lifestyle for the family and friends as well as the player; it's a reason for traveling to camps and games. When the player loses football, everyone in his sphere loses it too.

"I look back and see that I was hiding in the material world of the NFL," he explains. "I was hiding behind big muscles, a nice car, and 'Hey, I'm an NFL player!' But sooner or later, God will cut you down. I listen to a lot of Johnny Cash."

Schmitt is now an accomplished, self-taught nature and landscape photographer, garnering media interviews (for the photography) and appearing in art galleries. "God tore the ego off of me," he says. "I got introduced to Mother Nature. Out there is ultimate truth."

Schmitt looks different today than he did in the thick-necked, hard-ass San Diego State days. On the rare occasions that he photographs himself, the image is of a bearded, slightly unkempt traveling artist, with smaller deltoids and biceps covered in tattoos. It is the image of the recovering football player.

His work ranges from the occasional rare cityscape (like a shot of an LA sunset) to snow-capped mountain ranges and secluded waterfalls. Occasionally Schmitt adds his own prose to the shot, such as his meditation on the Columbia River Gorge, in Oregon: "Consciousness has shifted. One by one people are opening their new eyes to the realization that nothing is relevant but that which is built upon truth. All that is constructed with unjust intention will once again be washed anew. Cleansed through nature's will. Have a great Sunday friends, always remember to live the *truth*."

Schmitt shoots all over the country but says he feels most at home shooting in Hawaii and Oregon. He says it has taken a while for the people in his life to get used to his new persona. "My folks support my photography now," he explains. "But you know how people are . . . it's not until you actually have some success that people believe in you."

Schmitt travels alone when he is working. "I can use my own intuition," he says. "I've met people from around the world. It's my favorite thing about the work."

"I've been sleeping in the back of my car for the past week and a half, chasing light for hundreds of miles up and down the coast with not much luck," he wrote on his Instagram page. "On my return trip home last night Mother Nature finally decided I had put in the work needed to capture a piece of her glory. Here's a shot of lightning striking the Village of La Jolla from the Torrey Pines Glider Port."

It's fitting that a player in perhaps the game's most solitary position has taken on such a solitary career. I ask him, semi-cliché-ishly if he misses the game, and he begins to give a semi-cliché-ish answer ("I miss the guys," blah, blah) before catching himself.

"I don't think about it every day," he says. "But when I was a football player I was always surrounded by people. I had more friends than I could count. But sometimes, now, I just think 'Dude, where'd everyone go?'"

❊ ❊ ❊

There was a recent column on SB Nation about how all teams carry a regular, exclusive long snapper now—that's not a surprise—but also how many teams have no real contingency plan for if that snapper gets hurt. To wit, the Raiders long snapper Jon Condo was injured recovering a fumble in their game against Denver this week, and rather than attempt a Condo-less extra point, the team opted to try for a two-point conversion. The column went on to chronicle several other instances, in recent memory, in which teams were relatively screwed without their starting snappers.

Columnist Rodger Sherman wrote,

- In 2012, Oakland's Jon Condo got a concussion and had to leave the team's Week 1 game against San Diego. Travis Goethel, a rookie linebacker who hadn't snapped in a game since high school, filled in. *He failed massively.* His first snap skipped to Shane Lechler, who bobbled it and was tackled. On the second, Lechler lined up just 12 yards back to make the snap easier, but the punt was blocked. On the third, the ball bounced multiple times and was never cleanly fielded. San Diego would kick three field goals after the snapping failures, and won by eight points.
- In 2008, Pittsburgh's Greg Warren tore a knee ligament against the Giants. Multi-time Pro Bowl linebacker James Harrison filled in, his first ever game action at snapper. *His only snap sailed over punter Mitch Berger's head for a game-tying safety .* The ensuing free kick gave New York the ball at their own 47-yard line, and they scored a game-winning touchdown on the short field.

- When long snappers do get injured, teams often go to great lengths to avoid playing their backups. Washington's Nick Sundberg broke his arm in 2012 during the first half of a game against the Saints. *He played the second half,* because a long snapper with a broken arm is often better than a non-long snapper with two completely intact arms.[1]

To me, this all puts my friend Jon Akemon's quest into sharper focus. There are so few of these jobs available, and he is locked in an internal battle over whether to continue throwing currency—emotional and actual—at the dream. He has decided to travel to Mobile, Alabama, to try out at one of Michael Husted's camps that, like Gary Zauner's, give guys like Jon the opportunity to be "charted" and to work out in front of scouts from the NFL and CFL. According to Husted's site,

The kicking camp will include:

- Up to three days of charting and evaluations
- Two days of instruction
- Two days of video
- Small group sessions to ensure quality

The benefits for free agents:

- To let objective data through our NFL style workouts be used to showcase your talent
- Receive professional instruction from former NFL players and coaches that have over 50 years of experience
- Valuable consultation on what it takes to perform at a high level and position yourself for opportunities
- A chance to qualify to kick in front of NFL, and CFL coaches and player personnel

Over the years, dozens of athletes from our camps have been signed to professional contracts in the NFL, CFL and arena leagues. Many Pro teams rely on us to provide them with current information on prospects and free agents.

"Wanna go to Mobile?" Akemon texts. I don't know how to respond. I do want to, kind of. The Husted camp is during Senior Bowl week, which is one of my favorite events on the NFL calendar and is a veritable feeding frenzy for NFL coaches, administrators, scouts, and hangers-on. The Husted camp would also be a very cool experience for this book, yet it's expensive, and I'm not sure I'm physically (or financially) ready for that kind of commitment. Still, it's appealing inasmuch as it would be used to feed the Dream. The point being, for guys like Akemon (and me), it's not so much even about what *happens* at a camp like this but only that it is scheduled, on the calendar, to be dreamed about, and to be trained for.

I decide to write Husted, to see if he'll let me come down and snap, and as I write, a familiar nerves-meets-excitement feeling wells up in my chest—the million to one shot that says, "What if I snapped incredibly well and it *went somewhere?*"

Husted writes back within twenty-four hours extending, graciously, the invitation to come and snap for a couple of pro coaches at the camp. I'm kind of shocked, then nervous, and then excited. Like Akemon, I now have emotional currency invested and a new sense of purpose to my workouts. Through all the discussions with arena teams, semi-pro teams, and random personnel people, this is the most concrete opportunity yet.

I drive onto campus and have the best workout—weights, snapping, running, and plyometrics—I've had in a month.

We'll both be going to Mobile, and we'll both be nervously wondering if it will Go Somewhere. Though as I ponder this, reading through an old *ESPN the Magazine* feature by Seth Wickersham on former 49ers general manager Scot McCloughan, I wonder about the validity of this "dream" in the first place. There's an old adage in the NFL that either you're an alcoholic or you're Born Again. The piece is an in-depth chronicle of McCloughan's alcoholism, but it could be anybody because it's not so much about alcohol as much as it's about what happens when living your dreams doesn't make you happy. McCloughan, in a worldly and NFL-related sense, had everything. He had plenty of money, was making personnel decisions, and was running a team. He had total control and yet, in spite of all of the above, was miserable in his own head. Most poignantly, the piece wrote that McCloughan, one Christmas morning, drove into the office after opening presents, out of some skewed sense of obligation. He was, the piece explained, feeling guilty about not being at home when he was at work and guilty about not being at work when he was at home.

The whole thing is a chilling reminder that "having" football, at whatever level, is not in any way an "answer." It could be an enjoyable thing, and it can provide some memories, but it will not fix what's fundamentally wrong with us.

* * *

I meet Glenn Pakulak in person between Christmas and New Year's. We meet at a pizza place in Howell, halfway between Lansing, where I'm staying, and his home in Detroit. Glenn rolls up in another vintage Cadillac—this one a little bit less pristine and a little bit less awesome than the one he had in New Orleans. This is the vintage ride of someone operating on a budget but still with impeccable style. The vanity plate reads "MOYO," which stands for "Motown Over Yo'Town," something of a personal mantra for Pakulak, and the brand name of his new apparel company. His days are spent approving designs, communicating with manufacturers, and evaluating fabrics for the shirts and tote bags his company will eventually sell. The products are all, he explains, made in America.

Pakulak and I are trying to make a movie. He has read my script—about an ex-USFL quarterback who leaves his comfortable suburban life to go and live as a squatter in the old Pontiac Silverdome. The dome gets more trashed with each passing day and is just the sort of bombed-out and haunted-looking locale that Ty Schmitt would enjoy photographing. To say that Glenn is enthusiastic about the script would be an understatement. His excitement is infectious, and as we scarf down pizza with my two sons, we all soon feel as though it's just a matter of time before we're collecting our Oscars.

My son is wearing a Patriots sweatshirt, and before long, it is the subject of a deep bond between Pakulak and him. "I love Danny Amendola," Tristan explains.

"No way! I lived with Danny in Dallas," Glenn replies.

"My favorite player on defense is Rob Ninkovich," says Tristan.

"No way! Rob and I hung out all the time when we were with New Orleans!" Glenn says. Ninkovich originally tried to make the Saints as a long snapper. He also begged his coaches for the opportunity to play some linebacker and was summarily dismissed. All he has done is go to New England and hold down the position for a decade—a human embodiment of the reminder that football is a team game and a less freakish guy who is doggedly determined and utterly dependable can still win championships and live dreams. We hope to be the film version of Rob Ninkovich. We are chipping away at it, slowly but surely, securing our first investors and locations. There is, still, the issue of the woman who will star alongside Glenn. We run through a litany of nineties' actress names—women we admired when we were young but who will be the perfect age now. Ione Skye (from *Say Anything*), Candace Cameron (from *Full House*), and even Winona Ryder (from the nineties in general).

"What was the name of the girl who played Winnie Cooper in *The Wonder Years*?" Glenn asks, furiously punching at his phone. Her name is Danica McKellar.

"Dude, how crazy would it be if we could get Winnie?"

Winnie. Her name will become a rallying cry in future weeks. When we're feeling down about the progress we're making, we will simply text *Winnie*.

We hug good-bye in the parking lot, and Glenn exchanges high fives with my sons.

"That guy was awesome," Tristan says, slamming shut the door of our own not-quite-vintage Caddy.

✵ ✵ ✵

The e-mail from R. J. Gabaldon, from the Windy City Ravens, comes nearly a year after I first contacted them. They are an arena team in the Chicago area, and are interested in my project. I dial RJ and find him to be bright, articulate, and like me, old.

"There are a few guys on the team in their upper thirties," he explains. This is music to my insecure ears. RJ is an investment banker and moonlights as the Ravens starting quarterback. Like me, he appears to be doing this for reasons that are no longer pragmatic (i.e., financial or glory related) but rather existential. I feel an immediate connection and, after all the fits and starts, feel certain that this is the team for which I'll suit up.

Given the immediacy of this commitment—we play in six weeks—I begin snapping in pads on a regular basis. I have always loved the feeling of sliding the pads over my shoulders. It has been written about ad nauseam, but it really is gladiatorial. I select a black Adams A200 helmet that I last wore in 2006 as a member of the Battle Creek Crunch. I will remove the Crunch decals and replace them with the Ravens logo. The helmet is lighter than its Schutt and Riddell brethren, and I always liked the fit and feel of it. Though it performed abysmally in the Virginia Tech concussion study, I am hopeful that I won't be colliding much and decide to wear it anyway.

The impending game brings back the old, nerved-up feelings.

"In a game of failure, coached by negative people, in a misinformation environment, you have to create your own confidence," explains former major league pitcher and current performance guru Tom House, in Bruce Feldman's book on NFL quarterbacking. "If you have a bad process, but end up with a good outcome, you're lucky." This was me, for most of my long snapping career. My process wasn't necessarily bad all the time; it just wasn't consistent.

"Stress is a ten-pound load for a five-pound box," House explains. "Anxiety is hormonal. Stress is physical. Anxiety is adrenaline and all that good stuff. You want to be a little anxious. It's the feeling you miss the most. When you're walking between those lines and you're going EREREAAAA! That doesn't happen in the real world. Choking is thinking too much, and panicking is not thinking enough."

Today I'm anxious about my purple toe: pinkie, right foot. It feels juvenile to say the word "pinkie." I stubbed it on New Year's Eve, when I was crashing at my buddy Steve's house. A dark and narrow staircase leading from the attic—home to Xboxes and a giant television—was the culprit. As it turns out, childish pursuits (Xbox, etc.) might end up putting a serious damper on my childish pursuits (football).

The Union University athletic training professor wiggles it in a way that has real "this little piggy went to market" connotations. I tell him I've had trouble keeping an ice pack on it, to which he replies, "Got a bucket?" He suggests a total submersion ice bath. "It'll be great," he explains. "I mean, it'll suck, but it'll be great."

It's good to be talking with an athletic trainer, whose job it is to get and keep athletes on the field. It's good, weirdly, to be sitting in a training room, on an exam table. It makes me feel young again. Husted's camp is five days away.

Honestly, the injury thought is never far from my mind, and being in dialogue with the Ravens has brought it all up again. The Husted thing will be completely safe—just snapping in shorts—but the Ravens thing, what with the actual combat, causes some reflection on old injuries.

When I broke my collarbone as a semi-pro player and sat in the emergency room at Lansing Sparrow Regional Hospital, I thought about how ridiculous I must have looked shirtless (they had to cut my jersey off) and in football pants, while the other clients in the room were mostly children there to get stitches. A morbidly obese doctor sniffed derisively at my predicament, and I in turn sniffed derisively at his physique. The surgery was miserable and left a two-inch scar on my right clavicle, a scar that to this day feels weird when touched.

"I'm damaged goods," I said sadly to my wife, as though this were news to her, as though I could power through life on a cloud of achievement and raw masculine sexuality and somehow fool her into thinking that I was a perfectly awesome guy. "I knew that before," she replied, not unkindly and in a statement that encompassed a lot, both physically and spiritually: damaged goods, from day one. Determined to prove that the broken collarbone would not keep me down, I went to the beach the next day. I threw up when I got home.

They shaved half my chest for the surgery, and I shaved it the rest of the way—something I'd always wanted to do. My wife walked in on me shaving and says that I had a sheepish look on my face like the kind of sheepish look children get when they're caught doing something bad. "Let it grow back," she said. "It's like sleeping with an adolescent."

She bought me a tacky recliner to convalesce in, and friends brought over stacks of football magazines, even though football was the thing that had gotten me here in the first place.

✮ ✮ ✮

The scar on my right leg was red and angry looking for a long time. Underneath it is a metal plate and ten screws and also part of the bone from my ankle, which the doctor assured me would grow back. I was seventeen when I broke my fibula during a Wednesday practice, and after sitting in the Blackford County Hospital emergency room watch-

ing *Batman* reruns, the doctor finally put an air cast on it and said it
would be fine. The surgery—performed by the Indianapolis Colts team
surgeon—involved rebreaking the roughly set leg and grafting in some
bone from my ankle.

My friend Russell, trying to make me feel better about the crutches,
said "Dude, your triceps are going to get huge." A nice cheerleader
carried my books from class to class.

Again, my friends brought over football magazines—exactly the
thing that had gotten me here in the first place.

I reflect on all of this as I pack for the Husted camp—a week early.
"I just don't want to embarrass myself," I explain to my friend Cory. "I
don't want to be a joke."

16

MOBILE AND THE NATURE OF EMBARRASSMENT

Mitchell's Barbershop in my hometown had one chair, located centrally at the front of the room, in front of a giant mirror and in front of the combs floating in jars of a fascinating radioactive blue liquid called "Barbicide." A tricolor rotating barber pole was out front, and it was situated adjacent to the library, which came by way of a Carnegie grant and was the nicest building in our town, by a long shot. Mitchell would put you in the chair and then affix the cape and begin asking a series of completely harmless nice-old-guy questions, such as about school and peewee football and about whether I wanted a shave (ha, ha—I'm seven). But the problem, for a pathologically introverted and completely awkward little kid was that the rest of the room was full of grizzled, blue-collar Hartford City men—farmers, factory guys, and guys in John Deere hats with leathery skin and steely-eyed gazes—men that would just stare intently at me while I stammered out answers to Mitchell's totally harmless line of questioning. The whole thing was so exhausting for introverted seven-year-old me that I would race out of Mitchell's and immediately abscond to the farthest reaches of the library where I could be alone with a book for long stretches of time. "I like how the library smells," I would tell my mom. This was the beginning of a life of uncool introversion.

I hated getting my haircut at Mitchell's for the same reason I now hate snapping in front of a bunch of NFL coaches and big-time college players. I'm in Mobile, Alabama, for Michael Husted's Free Agent Pro

Tryout camp, on a muddy field early in the morning, and am snapping an official NFL ball in front of a bunch of official NFL people. Mitch Palmer played for the Tampa Bay Bucs and the Minnesota Vikings. Justin Snow played for the Colts and the Redskins. Kyle Stelter had a cup of coffee in a Jets minicamp. They're all coaches now. Joining them, standing in a semicircle around me, are (in no particular order) the snapper from Auburn last year, the snapper from Auburn now, and former snappers from Indiana University, Purdue University, the Chicago Bears, and a smattering of small colleges including Franklin (I was recruited by them, a lifetime ago), Northern Michigan (they play football in a wooden dome), and Assumption (whose name I've always loved because it is a noun for the act of "assuming").

My legs are shaking. The fertilizer on the field smells like hot perm. It's thirty-three degrees and I'm realizing, just now, that there's a world of difference between snapping on a muddy field with an NFL ball and snapping in a gymnasium with a college ball. As Tupac once sang, All Eyes Are On Me. Just like at Mitchell's Barbershop.

❊ ❊ ❊

In July 1860 a slave ship called the *Clotilde* (a French form of a Germanic word meaning something about "fame" and "battle") entered Mobile Bay. Its cargo was ferried onto a riverboat and hustled ashore before the *Clotilde* was set ablaze. This was over a half century after the slave trade had been outlawed by the United States. The hundred or so Africans aboard were taken to shore, where they were stripped, evaluated, and eventually sold to the parties who had bought into the shady little venture on the front end.

Today, elite college football players fly into Mobile with their agents from places like Los Angeles, California, and Ann Arbor, Michigan. They collect bags, rent cars, and make their way to the Mobile Convention and Visitor's Bureau downtown, which is a large steel-and-glass structure that boasts a breathtaking view of the selfsame bay where they set fire to the *Clotilde*. The last time I was here I was in the penthouse suite, being condescended to by the family of legendary American Tim Tebow.

Today I'm sitting in gridlock in front of the bureau because, as I'll find out, a Mobile Mardi Gras float has capsized—slid off the flatbed trailer hauling it—and now lays sadly on its side in the middle of the road. A sad reminder that, from a Mardi Gras standpoint, this is no New Orleans.

Today the athletes will disembark, check in, be assigned numbers, and then, at the pinnacle of day one of the Reeses Senior Bowl, strip to their underwear and parade across the stage where they will be evaluated (turn to the right, to the left, arms out) by the entities who will eventually purchase their services. Said entities will make comments about their bodies such as "small hands" or "a little smooth." These comments will go a long way toward setting their market value.

Making this juxtaposition—the *Clotilde* and the Reeses Senior Bowl (named, ironically, after a popular brand of fattening candy)—is a cheap and kind of college-sophomorish shock-value thing to do. It's obviously an apples-to-oranges kind of comparison in that in the case of the Reeses Senior Bowl, the participants don't have to be there and are poised, in some cases, to make very large sums of money. Also, in the case of the Senior Bowl, they're not all black.

* * *

Husted's affair is, by comparison, much lower key. We're housed in a Holiday Inn Express in a suburb named "Daphne," whose name evokes images of pleasant-looking 1980s girls. The lobby is a who's who of eighties and nineties special-teams standouts—names such as Louie Aguiar, Mike Hollis, Husted himself, and the gigantic Australian punter Darren Bennett. Husted's camp is for snappers, punters, and kickers. There is no requirement to strip to one's underwear and parade anywhere, but the performance anxiety is similar.

It occurs to me that these players—all of whom were college stars and many of whom have already been in NFL training camps—are the best that our gene pool has to offer: tall, broad shouldered, interesting looking, affluent enough to be here, and confident, all of them. The swag around the room, at the moment, includes Georgia, Houston, Florida State, and something called the Famous Idaho Potato Bowl, which is a college bowl game sponsored by the Famous Idaho Potato Company and that featured Ohio University. There's a guy who was in a minicamp with the Jets who will wear his Jets swag every waking moment he is here, as though every trip to the lobby is a swag-fueled fashion show—the message being "I was once with the Jets and I'll wear this Nike Dri-Fit Jets shirt until it literally falls off me." I don't blame him. I'd do the same thing.

I explain to my wife that I can kind of identify what part of the country these athletes are from, just by the way they look. One small-school, Deep South snapper has the sort of tall, affluent chinlessness that one often sees in the stands at Ole Miss games, with the swooped-over hair and bow tie. It's a look that says, "My dad is in investment banking." The upper-midwestern kids all look . . . upper midwestern. Their faces have stubble, and they pull their skullcaps down low. The West Coast kids have floppy hair and wear tights under their shorts.

"I hate this," my wife explains, over hotel-lobby eggs.

What she means is that she hates the macho guy culture: swaggering, posturing, and competing. "I love/hate it," I respond, staring at my own hotel eggs, already neck deep in fear and insecurity. The fact is, I respect this process. I respect the fear. I don't want to live a life without fear because when I do live that life I very quickly get bored. In a few minutes I'll say good-bye to her, get in my car, and drive to the field, where I'll (for one morning) be competing with these twenty-two-year-old marvels of genetics and training. I love it and hate it at the same time. I hate the risk of embarrassment—just as at Mitchell's when I had grown men staring at me, watching me fail. The thought makes me sick to my stomach.

I hop in the car and call my dad. "What are you going to do, clothing wise, to look younger?" he asks. He is sixty-seven and still playing beer-league ice hockey. Denial runs in my family.

"I think that ship has sailed, Pops."

Being in the presence of these genetic heroes, and driving through rural Mississippi the day before, has caused a lot of reflection on entropy and loss. What few towns and buildings we encountered in rural Mississippi all seemed to be trophies of decay. Stated simply and inarticulately, it was really sad—and lonely. We drove hours between tiny towns. When we stopped in a town called Citronelle, and went inside a McDonalds, we were gawked at as though we had just stepped in from a different planet. In all of our travels through eastern and western Europe, we were never gawked at in such a way.

I gawk at my own aging body in a similar way, especially in light of my competitors here. I am sliding downhill, while they are still rising.

My wife and I talked about sex, on the way down. "I don't want to be one of those sexless, platonic older couples who are just really good friends," she explains.

The football, in a weird way, is a big part of this for me. As long as I'm still playing, I can still think of myself as a virile, competitive, and *dangerous* individual. I can think of myself as the antithesis of the khaki-pantsed, turtlenecked, dad-jeaned lame ass I so fear becoming. If I were a woman, I wouldn't want to have sex with that person. I want to stay attractive to my wife, and in my skewed sense of reality, this is part of it.

I exit the car next to Justin Snow, who will be my coach for the morning. He played a dozen years in the NFL and still looks as if he could walk right out onto a field and snap. He appears taller than the six foot three in the program. Perhaps this is just the intimidation talking. He manages to be truly nice without really being especially curious about my project. I spend more than a little time thinking about how this is possible. Actually, it's completely understandable from his perspective. Why would anyone, necessarily, want to go through the indignity of being an amateur snapper trying to compete with professionals? He probably has an inkling that what I'm about to do is going to be really humbling. He's right.

Inside the gate—this is a high school field in a residential neighborhood—I meet Kyle Stelter, who will end up being a sort of intellectual and emotional tour guide for the next three hours. He has a friendly face and a Wisconsin accent. This, I find, puts me at ease. I learn that he played at the University of Wisconsin at River Falls and is himself a graduate of the Husted Camps, where he snapped successfully enough to be invited to a New York Jets minicamp.[1]

When people describe other people as "great," what they're describing is Stelterian: eye contact, good humor, actual listening, and a sense of helpfulness that is in no way condescending.

It's cold. The grass field is muddy under a patina of frost. Players are scattered about in various states of "warm-up." Some listen to music, some pace, and some snap incessantly. Some of the more blessed athletes look completely relaxed. Brandon Hartson snapped at the University of Houston and most recently with the Chicago Bears. Being the most accomplished snapper in our group, he has the look of the cool high school senior. His clothes fit better. His swagger is more complete.

He wears an earring and a headband and totally pulls it off. His snaps are perfect. He is treating this as I treat a day in my classroom: simply a pro doing his work and, on a good day, doing it with flourish and swag. Teaching writing is as fun and easy for me as snapping is for Hartson. I am full of envy.

I shake hands with Mitch Palmer, whose hands feel gigantic and meaty. Palmer's head and neck seem to be one. He asks me how I want to go about "charting," which is the agenda item for the morning. In charting, snappers are asked to snap for punts and field goals, and are videotaped doing so. The charting is later watched and evaluated by Stelter, Snow, and Palmer.

A stocky kid who played fullback at the University of Ohio before a stint as a linebacker at the University of Rhode Island paces around and mutters curse words under his breath. "I feel like I'm gonna fucking puke," he says, to no one in particular. He is nervous and has the neurotic disposition that is actually helpful for the fullback/linebacker. I share this. It's the difference between being a hog butcher and a heart surgeon. Both work with knives. Both cut meat. But the butcher is doing large-scale damage, while the heart surgeon deals heavily in preparation and fractions of inches. Same for the long snapper.

"Please don't make this moment bigger than it is," says Snow. "It's just another day to snap." This is the kind of untrue but nurturing thing that coaches say to make players feel better. He is right, in a sense. But in another sense guys have made big investments to be here, and there is a lot on the line. In the same conversation: "Scouts can read body language. This is supposed to be fun."

Right now the moment is feeling pretty huge for me. I stretch. Finally I work up the courage to find a guy to catch some warm-up snaps for me. His name is Jake David, and he snapped at tiny Franklin College in Indiana. We kill time by chatting about Indiana and the recruiting methods germane to the small, NCAA Division III school whose business model seems to be to recruit as many athletes as possible as a means of keeping tuition dollars flowing.

"We had fifty-five strong in my freshman class," he explains. "We finished with eighteen, and that was considered good."

I can hear former NFL punter Louie Aguiar telling stories from across the field. He's recounting tales of life in a pre-dedicated-snapper NFL. "In 1993 I had seventy-three punts . . . twenty-six were bad snaps.

I was fielding them all over the place! What are you looking at, Kyle?" he shouts in our direction. Kyle smiles. "I'm pretty entertaining . . . I should have my own f——king reality show!" The f-bomb is less a pejorative and more just a way of life for current and former football players. It can be a verb, an adjective, and a noun, and is living proof of the kind of protracted adolescence all football people live in, which is, on one level, super appealing. Even the coaches get to, for a time, live a life that consists of hotel rooms, meals with their buds in chain places, and beers in the evenings: guffawing, memory sharing, and ball busting. Most of us, as we slide into responsible and respectable middle age, have to leave all of that behind.

When it's time for me to snap, I settle in and fire two solid warm-up snaps, but as soon as the camera rolls, adrenaline kicks in and I sail a ball over the punter's head. In a sense, my worst fear is coming to bear: screwing up in front of a bunch of people whose respect I desire. I take a deep breath and settle in. "We'll start with this one," says Palmer, trying to calm my frayed nerves.

The rest of my snaps are serviceable—a little wobbly and almost all low but fieldable. I'm low because I'm overcompensating due to my fear of another high snap. Mercifully, it ends after a few moments, and the fear is replaced by a momentary flush of euphoria at being done. What's helpful is that all of the pros in the area don't really seem to care. They're all, rightfully, absorbed in their own heads.

"It's obvious you can snap," says Palmer. "Ten minutes together, and we'd get all this stuff fixed." He is being kind, I think, but I feel hopeful that there's a grain of truth in it. What's encouraging is that even though my snaps weren't always accurate, they were pretty fast. Many were in the .70s; a few of the wobblier ones, in the .80s.

After a few moments I am over the ball again, preparing for my field-goal snaps. Part of the delicate psychic/emotional dance of this whole thing is the issue of finding a holder, which gets into some pretty deep-seated high school, who-am-I-sitting-with-at-lunch kinds of fears. "Can anybody hold for me?" asks the former fullback at Ohio. Nobody volunteers, and it's excruciating. Everybody just shuffles around with their heads down. I realize I need to spring into action to get this important piece taken care of for myself, lest I'm wandering around aimless in the same way.

"Dude, can you hold for me?" I ask Jesse Medrano. He was a snapper at the University of Texas at San Antonio. I ask Medrano if he's receiving any nibbles from teams.

"My issue is my height," he explains. He's around five foot ten but otherwise solidly built and a good snapper. He works at Olive Garden but moonlights as a snapping instructor for coach Kyle Stelter, whom he refers to as "my owner." Stelter, I'm sure, would be at least put off by, if not outright horrified at, the thought of being referred to as anyone's owner. Happily for me, he agrees to catch my field-goal snaps.

The chinless southern-affluence guy is struggling. He's low on all his snaps, it seems, because his left (or guide) hand is doing pretty much nothing besides falling off the ball—also probably because he's (understandably) very nervous. Stelter explains that my guide hand should be more involved, even to the degree of being able to palm the football with it if my right hand is completely removed from the equation. He then explains the differing schools of thought vis-à-vis placement of the guide hand at all. I put the middle finger of my left hand on the seam. Jake David, from Franklin College, has his guide hand way down low. There seems to be no hard and fast "right" interpretation here, so the guide hand will remain something of a mystery.

What is surprisingly true of Chinless/Affluent but also some other guys here—including Ohio Fullback—is that they've been out of school for quite a while. Chinless and Fullback have both been out since 2013. One of my favorite guys, a friendly snapper named Tyler Kruzel, has been out of school since 2010 and is now working a legitimate career as a high school administrator. His Northern Michigan University gear is starting to look a little faded, as the years have gone by.

There's a sort of next level of confidence exuded by the guys who have spent any amount of time in the NFL, like Hartson, and like Trevor Gillette, who was with the Jacksonville Jaguars for a little while. They walk a little taller. Their jokes are a little funnier. They're given a little bit wider breadth around here, even by the coaches, for whom the unspoken mutual-respect hierarchy is thrown momentarily out of balance by their presence.

Gillette is listed at six foot three and 240 pounds. If he is either, then I am six foot five and 270 (I'm not). He looks slight, but his snaps are perfect. He played high school football on a team that went 46–0 while he was a member of it, and he actually played some defensive end at

Rice too. He has the look and bearing of the preternaturally gifted athlete. I am too deep into my own anxiety to chat him up. That said, almost everyone I meet at this thing ends up being genuinely cool.

What's weird about all of this too is how quiet it is. Really at any given time there are only the sounds of footballs hitting hands, thudding off of feet, and then hitting the ground. Occasionally words are spoken, but they're the exception. There are very few conversations happening, but more start happening as guys finish the tense part of the morning and are feeling less burdened. There is the occasional shout of "incoming!" which indicates that a punter has accidentally shanked a ball into our area. This is rare, because the punters are really good too. I only meet one punter, a kid named Matt Wile from the University of Michigan, whose father, grandfather, and great-grandfather all graduated from the UM Medical School, which I assume must place an ungodly amount of pressure on the thin shoulders of one Matt Wile.

"Do you know how to snap laces?" Palmer asks shortly before my field-goal snaps. We collect Medrano and move to a section of field where I bend down and fire two or three perfect field-goal snaps. This is good. I'm feeling something akin to actual confidence, which is a nice feeling that I haven't had much of.

Palmer explains that where I place the ball on the yard line (butt of ball on line?) will determine where to place Medrano so that the ball will hit his palm at the perfect number of rotations such that the laces will face "out," making a smoother experience for the kicker. How he can intuit this is a mystery to me in the same way that all remarkable things are a mystery to the people who can't do them. I'm feeling pretty good.

When I settle the ball for my first field-goal snap, it is wobbly and low. I'm nervous about firing it over the holder's head.

"You're old enough to remember Inspector Gadget?" Snow asks. I am, sadly, old enough for that. "Imagine yourself Go-Go-Gadget-arming the ball back to the holder." This is a kind way to tell me to follow through with my hands to the target. There are two schools of thought at play here, Stelter explains. There are the "release point" people, who preach a consistent release point each time, which seems (to me and, as it turns out, to Stelter) a completely arbitrary and impossible thing to replicate from snap to snap. Then there are the follow-through people who preach that it is following through with hands to the target that makes for the perfect snap. This makes more sense intuitively.

The rest of my field-goal snaps are what I would call "decent": not as good as in practice but serviceable. This gives me at least a modicum of confidence as I strip off my perm-smelling cleats and make my way back to the car. A feeling of intense relief washes over me. It's the kind of relief that one feels immediately following something miserably nerve racking. This speaks to personality, because I think not everyone at the stadium feels as miserable about this as I do.

❀ ❀ ❀

In my real, nonfootball, life, I am a frequenter of the Myers-Briggs Personality Inventories (MBPI). I find them useful in the classroom as I try to figure out my students and what motivates them. In the MBPI, the user takes a short exam and is given a four-letter profile. Mine is INFP, which means "introverted, intuitive, feeling, and perceiving." It is basically the "brilliant, suicidal writer" profile, if the celebrities who share my profile are any indication. We have people like Kurt Cobain, Ian Curtis (Joy Division), Virginia Woolf, and Sylvia Plath. INFPs are known as idiosyncratic dreamers with strong imaginations. INFPs can be great artists but also sometimes suck horribly at the practical aspects of life.

I posit a theory over breakfast to Stelter that there might be an "ideal" Myers-Briggs type for snappers and then explain that I'm almost certain it's not mine. Football coaches are a great many things, good and bad, but most of them are naturally curious about anything that can help them achieve their goals. Stelter agrees to take the exam and text me the results.

"I'm ISTJ," he texts, not long after our conversation. This type is referred to as "the logician," which is not surprising given Stelter's obsession with breaking down snapping film and noticing things the rest of us wouldn't. Is the snapper using his full body? Are his knees over his toes? If so, he's too far forward. If the ball is already out by the time his knees are locked, he's robbing himself of power, and so forth.

ISTJs are known to be thorough and responsible. Stelter shares his type with guys such as George Washington, Ike Eisenhower, and Warren Buffet. This makes sense to me. There's little about snapping that engages my imagination; rather, it feels like a chore that could potentially go horribly wrong. I enjoyed linebacker and defensive end much more because each play offered a blank canvas of havoc-inducing potential. I could take an infinite number of angles to the ball carrier and then do creative and bad things to that ball carrier, things that could bring me fame and glory. Snapping is meant to be precise, anonymous, and replicated over and over. When it's working right, it's super boring. The INFP in me can't deal with the boring. It also can't deal very well with pressure and criticism.

"More results in," Stelter writes later. "Almost every good snapper I know is an ISTJ or ESTJ." Interesting. ESTJs are known as "no-nonsense, efficient organizers with a flair for practical logistics." This is my brother-in-law, an insanely successful engineer-turned-businessman for whom the term "practical logistics" was invented. My son is also an ESTJ and is a better snapper than me because he has no regard for what anyone thinks of him. This makes him a little insufferable at times in the home but pretty doggone compelling as an athlete. He has, simply, never been wrong. He snaps like a confident person because he is one.

I am full of envy.

17

BLOOMINGTON, ILLINOIS

Satisfaction versus Euphoria

I'm reminded that there are still, even in football, interpersonal relationships and those relationships can be difficult. "I suck horribly at all relationships," I say to my wife. "I give up." She knows I don't actually mean this but still. The introvert in me sometimes just wants to run for the hills and hide.

Even my short-lived blog writeup of Michael Husted's camp experience provided a lesson in humility, as I let my need for descriptive writing trump my need to actually be a decent human being. I had to apologize to someone, which is a humbling but oddly reassuring experience—reassuring because I'm realizing that even at nearly forty, I'm still growing.

I got a call from one of the coaches at the camp—whom I really respect—and he explained that something on my blog had hurt one of his snapping students who had himself had stints in NFL camps. Honestly, it hadn't occurred to me that this would be hurtful, but as soon as he called, I "got" it immediately. Interestingly, the call came during a tornado siren, which came while I was waiting in my car to pick up my son from school. The tornado felt like my life.

I changed the passage, because sometimes not hurting people is more important than being "authentic" or perfect at description. This I took as another sign that I might be maturing. Later, I spoke with Glenn Pakulak, the punter, and asked about Jon Akemon.

"He's getting a tryout with the Arizona Cardinals," he explained.

"Do you think he would be okay with me reaching out to congratulate him?" I asked.

I did reach out, and Jon's response was warm and gracious. We talked at length that day, and again after his successful workout in Arizona. He texted me pictures of his locker at the Cardinals facility and of the swag he got to wear. "What did they tell you?" I asked.

"They told me to stay by my phone." His voice was as hopeful as it had sounded in months.

o o o

It's 5:30 a.m., and I'm packing the car for my debut as a member of the Windy City Ravens professional indoor football team, which will occur later in the afternoon. I am, not surprisingly, a basket case of nerves, though I'm trying to show my wife that at nearly forty years of age, I am conquering this or at least getting out in front of it. She knows better and gamely tries to engage me in conversation on the drive, so that my mind isn't filled with "what ifs." The fact is, if I don't snap well, nothing disastrous happens. My life, my career, and even this book aren't really tied to my snapping performance. Still, I just *want* it. I want to be able to snap well, so that I can quit snapping. I need to do it in a game.

My parents—now in their late sixties—and my aunt are making the trip to Bloomington's U.S. Cellular Coliseum for the game. I can't help but be reminded of a game in high school, in which my Blackford Bruins played the Alexandria Tigers in the old Hoosier Dome (since renamed the RCA Dome, since torn down). It was a euphoric affair, with friends, family, and girls I liked filling the dome stands, me playing well, and then me exiting the dome with a head still wet from the shower, meeting adoring onlookers, and feeling utterly convinced that the rest of my life would feel like this. It hasn't.

I appeared on the front page of the next day's paper—again, euphoria.

In 1992 I listened to Metallica and Megadeth before games, in an attempt to infuse even more auditory testosterone into a teenage body already teeming with it. Today, I listen to hymns—church music—in an attempt to manage anxiety and remind myself of who I am: redeemed and worthwhile, regardless of what happens today.

My parents meet us in the dirty, trash-strewn parking lot of a some-what faded building nestled in the heart of a definitely faded Blooming-ton metro area. It is a grim, midwestern small city in the vein of Flint, Fort Wayne, Battle Creek, or Peoria—places with big-city problems, absent the big-city charm. My mom, for one, doesn't understand why on earth I am doing this, and why I put her in the strange position of having to enter a dirty arena, listen to loud hip-hop music, and wait three hours for a game to be over.

Interestingly, Bloomington is the former home of my favorite au-thor, David Foster Wallace, who lived there and taught at Illinois State University during the era shortly after his landmark novel *Infinite Jest* dropped. Like Wallace, I struggle with the life of the body/life of the mind tensions. While I love writing and academia, something inside me longs for combat and wants to be a badass forever. Something longs to connect with the kinds of tough, blue-collar people who live in Bloom-ington but don't work at Illinois State. We drove by the church where Wallace used to attend AA meetings.

Wallace, like me, was an INFP on the Myers-Briggs scale. So was, as it turns out, nearly every celebrity I've ever been attracted to (nonsexu-ally) or cared about—including Ricky Williams, Eddie Vedder from Pearl Jam, and Zach De La Rocha from Rage Against the Machine. This begged the question, in the car, "Are we destined to only really love or care about people who are just like us?"

I kiss my wife good-bye. It's time to go inside. The clack-clack of rolling-bag wheels on a sidewalk. The tall, gray walls of the dirty col-iseum. The blast of flat, Illinois wind. These are all semi-comforting.

"I feel kind of nervous, Dad," my son, Tristan, volunteers.

"I know, bud; I feel nervous too," I reply. Tristan will be with me through the whole ordeal, for which I'm thankful on a number of levels. The last time I did this he was just a toddler, and I'm sure he doesn't remember it. He's thirteen now, and like all fathers of thirteen-year-olds, I feel my little boy slipping away and am searching for ways to connect with him. I gave him the opportunity to be my documentary photographer for the afternoon, and he jumped at it.

I have to sweet-talk him past the horrifically unfriendly woman guarding the "VIP" entrance, which is as sad as you're probably imagin-ing the VIP entrance at this kind of place being. I notice the distinct lack of the kind of fake friendliness that I've grown accustomed to in the

South. We make it inside, together, and find the locker room with a sheet of paper emblazoned with "Ravens" taped to the door.

The locker room is empty. It's hockey-arena standard: rubber floor, benches around the walls, and crude hooks for your stuff. I imagined walking into a room full of teammates. This is off script and offers more time for reflection and nervousness.

Football, for me, is a primal reflection of myself. The aesthetics. I love the way this room looks. I love the way my helmet looks on the bench—shiny and black. I will love the way the jersey feels when pulled over my pads. I will miss all of this. I begin to get dressed.

I hang my "Motown Over Yo'Town" T-shirt on the hook and am aware of my aging, white torso. I quickly cover it with the shirt that goes under my pads. I slip on the black tights and the shiny black game pants. I am beginning to feel sleek and dangerous. We sit for a while in silence, just sipping water, and waiting for the team to arrive.

The young black guys begin to file in. "You playing with us today?" they ask. I affirm this. We bro-hug. Just like that, we're teammates. They know nothing of the book, or my age. They have muscly, tattooed bodies and the kind of practiced nonchalance that masks nervousness or, in some cases, terror. Head coach Petey Corriedo walks in and tosses me a gigantic purple jersey. It would be appropriate for William "the Refrigerator" Perry. I laugh and realize it has no number on it. It's one level below George Plimpton's famous "0" from *Paper Lion*. I laugh again.

Quarterback-slash-de-facto-coach R. J. Gabaldon enters the locker room, attired nattily in fashionable denim, cowboy boots, a cream-colored sport coat, and sunglasses. He is playing the role of the aging quarterback to perfection. This is the way he needs to look and, in fact, the way I wish I looked. There is nervousness in the locker room because of the fact that several of our teammates haven't arrived yet and won't, for a while.

Recently a friend (a black guy) explained "CPT" or "colored-people time," which is basically the concept wherein normal rules of when-to-show-up-related appropriateness don't really apply to people of color. "Just relax and go with it," he explained. "They'll show up. They always do."

I am the first one fully uniformed. There is a semi-pro game happening before ours, on the AstroTurf, and I can hear the tinny, canned arena music and cheers of the crowd through the concrete. Tristan and I make several trips into the hallway. At one point I grab a ball and snap a few practice field-goal snaps in his direction. When we return to the locker room, many of our linemen have arrived—they're huge. We average over three hundred pounds across the front, and our center, Nick Bledsoe, is fresh off a successful college career at Illinois State. He looks the part of the badass white dude and is deferred to in the way that all locker-room alphas are.

The crowd is . . . predictable. In the tunnel there are two guys leaning over the railing shouting down at us about how *they* should be the ones in uniform and how tough *they* are. Both of them, while posturing, have to dedicate one hand to holding up their sagging pants. I'm sure they are very impressive. Their girlfriends show their appreciation by yawning and staring at their phones. It's bizarre to be here and to be doing this.

Finally we get onto the field for warm-ups, and I hold while our kicker, Mike O'Brien, boots a few practice kicks through the narrow uprights. When I shook O'Brien's hand in the locker room I immediately recognized a kindred spirit. He has a kind face. I learn that he's a graduate student at Aurora University in the Chicago suburbs, studying for his master's in social work. He counsels kids and coaches special teams at Aurora High School. He's conflicted about this too, but he loves kicking and nurtures "the Dream." I have the utmost respect for this.

What's unique about our team, the Windy City Ravens, is that less than twenty-four hours ago, we played a game. In the modern era, doing this—playing back-to-back games on consecutive nights—is considered to be insanity bordering on suicidal. Football beats up the body in a way that makes scheduling like this prohibitive. The bodies of our players bear the marks—bruises and turf burns—of fresh combat. One of our guys has an elaborate bandage affixed to his neck. I approach Bledsoe about the long snapping for tonight, as none of this has been prearranged.

"Take it man," he says, of the snapping job. "I don't wanna even fuckin' play." He says this while leaning against the cinderblock wall, his eyes narrowed to slits. He looks really cool while saying this—like an endomorphic James Dean. I make my exit, excited and nervous both. All of the snapping will be on me tonight.

On the field for warm-ups I get exactly one snap with an official CIF game ball—a gaudy red, white, and blue Baden composite. For what it's worth, the snap is good. The ball is then repurposed for some passing drills, and at some point, I realize that I'm no longer nervous and am just having fun. It feels good to be doing this—running around on AstroTurf with young men. Up in the stands my wife is crocheting as the vestiges of hip-hop and young, raged-up men throb around her. She's a self-contained unit.

Regarding colored-people time: It has delivered for us big time in the form of Demetrius Jones, who was the third-rated quarterback, nationally, in his high school recruiting class behind Tim Tebow and Matthew Stafford. Jones, a Chicago prep superstar, signed with Notre Dame and started exactly one game for head coach Charlie Weis. He was benched that afternoon and replaced by super recruit Jimmy Clausen, whose story and personality are both well documented. After bouncing around the backcountry of college football, he wound up at Cincinnati, where he played linebacker just to get on the field. Finally, he is here, at the last outpost. He will keep us in the game tonight, leading our effort on both sides of the ball.

In keeping with the interesting hierarchy of eliteness in athletics, even though most of my teammates are quite talented and athletic, Jones is more so. He's just a little bit faster, smoother, and more relaxed. He's just better.

Regarding being better: Bloomington is better than we are. They have more players, just from a sheer numeric standpoint, and they have several Demetrius Joneses, to our one. As such, they jump out to a quick lead. When I snap for the first time I am doing so backed up against our own end zone. The whole scene plays out way more relaxed than I expect it to. The referee explains to the gigantic Bloomington linemen that they're not allowed to line up directly over me. I exhale, wipe my hands, pray silently ("Lord, I need you"), and bend down over the ball. I see R. J. Gabaldon, sans sunglasses. He shouts "down!" I wait a beat and then snap the ball. It's a little high but a tight spiral, right at the facemask.

As I jog off the field, I get a thumbs-up from Kristin and my dad. It's going to be okay. The rest of the evening unfolds in much the same way. It is neither exciting nor boring—in that, it is a lot like teaching or writing. Perhaps this is a function of my age. Every few plays I am pulling the helmet on over my dry, long hair and removing my gloves to trot out onto the field to snap. Often the most challenging thing is hopping over the padded wall. It's fun to run into the huddle—to realize I'm in a purple-jerseyed pro football huddle again; to see Gabaldon count the guys; and to settle over the ball, wipe my hands, and fire back another good snap. With each trip onto the field I feel more confident, and with each snap I get a little better until I realize, sometime in the second quarter, that I want to quit while I'm ahead. My last snap is my best, a rocket right into Gabaldon's hands at chest level.

As a specialist, you always feel a little guilty at halftime. Teammates are treating turf burns and guzzling water while you—relatively un-scathed—sit and reflect. It's a strange "in this but not *of this*" kind of feeling. I realize that I desperately want to play some defensive end, before it's all over. I also realize that this is it. This is the last football game I will ever play. The realization is not especially dramatic. It's just true. I have no desire to abuse my body and go home covered in open wounds anymore. I have no desire to break bones and sit in hospital waiting rooms. I've done that. But, one more time, I'd like to dig my gloved fingers into the turf and rush the quarterback.

I didn't do this in the first half for fear of taking another guy's "reps." But in the second half I go for it, bounding over the wall when a player calls for a rest. I line up at left defensive end and feel the rough turf beneath my gloved fingers. I look at the giant slab of meat lined up across from me. He is at least ten years my junior and probably out-weighs me by a hundred pounds. Still, he isn't fat. He looks scary. His stance is perfect. His arms have the requisite "bro" tribal tattoos. At the snap I explode out of my stance and drive my helmet into his. It hurts. The crowd cheers. Bloomington has scored. My series at defensive end lasted one play.

✲ ✲ ✲

We lose. I'm not sure of the score. I just know that I've snapped well and my dad has come down to the tunnel to greet me. My youngest son, Maxim, is there too. He's pumped because he has a souvenir football that has the name of a random defunct team (Trenton Freedom!) on it. Such is the not-quite-legitimate world of professional indoor football. Tristan shows me the beautiful photo essay he has compiled. The pictures are perfect—from our pregame meditations to the tunnel and the snaps themselves. I'm proud of him.

I am satisfied but not euphoric, which is, I think, what it feels like to be a full-fledged adult. In sixteen days I'll be forty years old. It has taken a long time to work out my adolescence with fear and trembling.

"Thanks so much for this, Coach," I say to Petey Corriedo.

"Feel free to join us for the rest of the season," he replies. I thank him but know in my heart that I won't. This has been what I've needed.

I pull off the helmet and pull my wife in close, for a hug and a kiss. Her warm, soft body feels perfect. She smiles and kisses me—gone are the threatened feelings and fears that I'll want to do this again.

Security guards open the gates, and kids pour onto the field. I find Tris and Maxim. They're such beautiful boys, and their heads are full of dreams. They explore the field and are soon running routes into the end zone. The last time I played arena football, Tristan was three years old. We were still wounded and in debt from his difficult Ukrainian adoption. Today he's nearly a man, at thirteen. I line up across from him and cover him as he runs a route into the end zone. Maxim, mimicking Demetrius Jones, lines up at quarterback. "Set, hut!" he shouts in his tiny little boy voice. Tris darts for the back corner of the end zone, and for a moment we are all who we think we want to be. We're all pro athletes.

The ball hangs in the air for a good, long time.

EPILOGUE

Major League

The most jarring thing about it is the silence—broken only by occasional laughter and the sound of packs of middle school kids chattering as they walk by.

"This is way more relaxing than football," I texted to my wife, as I sat in the grass, in the sunshine, in front of an open copy of David Foster Wallace's *Infinite Jest*, which is about (in part) tennis. I would glance up occasionally to see my son hit a ball and then keep score by placing a tennis ball in this little peg thing that is designed to hold tennis balls—the design of which struck me as brilliant in its simplicity.

I grew up in a hyper-aggressive football culture and had the chance to eventually play and coach the game at a pretty high level. In this culture the opponent was your "enemy" and you went to "war" on Friday night. In football culture you kept a "chip on your shoulder," "played angry," and "got after somebody." This was a culture where after a defeat it was a requirement to not smile and not laugh, and if there was a bus ride involved it was necessary to just stare out the window glumly, full of regret about how you didn't "leave it all on the field of battle."

Football was something you survived. I have enduring memories of two-a-days: bent over at the waist, sucking in gulps of air, and trying not to vomit up breakfast, or sitting on a concrete cleat-house floor with my body covered in bruises and open wounds, just staring blankly into space because all I had the energy to do was stare blankly into space. Don't get me wrong, this was cool—it was cool to be a survivor—but it also, quantifiably, really sucked.

I was always anxious and paranoid because I was afraid of losing and afraid of being embarrassed at a "war" that I felt meant way more than it actually did. I was, truth be told, afraid of getting hurt, which in football culture was a thing that you could never admit or talk about out loud. We listened to heavy metal or rap before football games because we were trying to prepare, mentally, to go and do a really counterintuitive thing—fight like men.

Here, at tennis, there is no rap, no metal, and no yelling. The coaches never raise their voices, and in fact, I can't even really tell who the coaches are because nobody is pacing around, frowning, and looking miserable. It's never really clear who the winners and losers are. There is no loudspeaker and no announcer praising the winner and shaming the loser.

"Are they playing yet or just warming up?" I ask the dad next to me. He is, as it turns out, the dad of my son's opponent. This is something that would never happen in football—opposing parents hanging out together. We laugh about how neither of us know anything about tennis and about how he took up tennis in college as a shameless ploy to meet girls.

"Because I don't know anything about this I can't ruin it for him," I explain to the other dad. He laughs because he knows exactly what I'm talking about.

I'm not antifootball. I think there's still a place for football, and toughness, in our culture. In fact, I still love it in the way that you still have affection for a really compelling lover who keeps hurting you but to whom you keep crawling back.

After football games, my parents' home was a triage ward. Bags of ice were dispensed, and wounds were cleaned and wrapped. After tennis, my son just tosses his bag in the car and starts chattering—high on victory and a fun afternoon with friends. I will always miss football, but this is really nice too.

※ ※ ※

I am teaching a spring-term writing course when I get the text from Tyler Kruzel. "Trever and I both got drafted by Major League Football. Unfortunately by the same team. Haha."

The text is very "him." I can see him tilting his head back and laughing from the belly at the irony of, on one hand, being a step closer to his dream and, on the other, having to battle it out with his brother for a job on an as-yet-unnamed team in a probably-won't-make-it league. Still, Tyler is the right person for a situation such as this. Where I would squeeze the situation to death with anxiety, he will show up, be everyone's friend by lunch on the first day, and make the best of it.

"Oh man, that is wild! And awkward?" I respond. "At any rate, congratulations!"

Major League Football (MLFB) is yet another quixotic attempt at a pro football minor league and is the brainchild of some people you've heard of. Its website has all of the right aggressive football photography (large doses of the color black) and says all of the right things regarding being fast paced and exciting, and for the fans and a new brand of pro football, in a way that makes all of it sound very, very old. The good thing about MLFB is that it creates a handful of additional snapping jobs for guys like Tyler and Trever.

Later, Jon Akemon simply texts me a screenshot from the MLFB site, indicating that he, too, has been drafted. It's a huge accomplishment, and I congratulate him accordingly. Out of all of the hundreds of guys on the camp circuit, Jon and the Kruzels have made it.

"I'm still hearing from NFL teams," Akemon texts. "MLFB will be a good thing. Several good snappers in that league. Hopefully I'm in preseason [in the NFL] somewhere, though."

He also, very kindly, asks, "How was your game?" I tell him that I snapped six times, all good, and even got to play a little on defense and kickoff return. "That's legit," he says. "Did you get any footage from that game you played in?" I respond that my son did take a video—one perfect snap, on a kick that ended up blocked. On the video, Tristan can be heard saying, "Oh my goodness!" as the Bloomington Edge defender slices through untouched to block the kick and send Mike O'Brien to the turf in a crumble of purple and black.

"That was a good snap by you," Akemon texts. This compliment feels really, really good.

Nate Boyer, never one to let the proverbial grass grow under his feet, has partnered with his roommate, Jay Glazer of Fox Sports, on the MVP Project—which as the acronym suggests, matches war veterans with players. "Warriors are a special breed," the site reads.

> They give of their body and spirit to causes greater than their own. They understand what it takes to achieve greatness. They represent excellence in all of its forms. They possess rare skills and abilities that are seldom seen in our society. They understand the meaning of words like selfless, service, teamwork, commitment, dedication, integrity, honor, performance and mission-focus. Warriors know that it is not what you say that matters—it is what you do. In short, Warriors are different—in the best ways possible.

"Both war fighters and football players need something to fight for once the uniform comes off, and your service to country or time on the field is over. Without real purpose for the man on your right and left, it can be easy to feel lost," said Boyer on the MVP site. Like all previous Nate Boyer projects—becoming an elite soldier, walking on at Texas, and playing in the NFL—I wouldn't bet against it.

Former NFL punter and reality TV star Glenn Pakulak continues to pursue his postfootball acting dream. He is slated to star in the independent film *Silverdome*, which will begin shooting in summer 2016. He also continues to be a fount of encouragement and good humor.

"I am doing well just trying to juggle between work, coaching, playing, and grad school," writes Mike O'Brien, kicker for the Windy City Ravens.

> However, I am enjoying everything that I'm doing. The team has had some difficulties retaining everyone after the tough weekend that we had. Demetrius Jones, the quarterback from Notre Dame, ended up signing with the Chicago Blitz and is no longer with us. The Blitz offered more pay and pay for travel so it was an offer that was good for him. The game in Denver ended up being cancelled so we are just practicing for our league games starting on April 2nd.

R. J. Gabaldon, investment banker, will resume the starting quarterback role as the Ravens begin league play.

Chicago-area long-snapping instructor Nolan Owen has once again joined forces with Chris Rubio, as his website is now branded as "Rubio

Long Snapping Instructor Nolan Owen." The partnership appears to be a "win-win" for all involved, as the site touts "22 & COUNTING RUBIO LONG SNAPPERS WHO ATTENDED WEEKLY LONG SNAPPING LESSONS UNDER NOLAN OWEN'S TRAINING PROGRAM HAVE MOVED ON TO PLAY DIVISION 1 COLLEGE FOOTBALL . . . HARD WORK PAYS OFF!" Owen's 2016 students include scholarship recipients at Notre Dame and Iowa State and preferred walk-ons at Purdue and Illinois.

Three snappers from the Husted Camp in Mobile have signed NFL contracts: Matt Dooley with the Pittsburgh Steelers, Brandon Hartson with the Dallas Cowboys, and Forrest Hill with the Indianapolis Colts.

☼ ☼ ☼

At Lane College they have what's called the Jacoby Jones Computer Laboratory, which is a space filled with technology funded, ostensibly, by former Lane College and NFL wide receiver Jacoby Jones, whose claim to fame is running a kickoff back for a touchdown in a Super Bowl while a member of the Baltimore Ravens. The space itself, in a place like this, delivers its own kind of weird tension in that while it is an institution of higher learning, a computer lab named after a football player just kind of reinforces the dream of being discovered, signed to an NFL contract, and then one day having your name on a wall at your university. It speaks to a little bit of permanence in a very impermanent world.

I'm here at Lane to talk about my journalism career, and I do so in a classroom full of Lane communications students—some of whom are football players. Their questions are incredibly insightful. I shared with them about my football addiction, the aborted college career, and the long journey through semi-pro and indoor experiences. There is some laughter, and the football players in the room can relate to the idea of the sport being one's sole identity and sole source of joy—and of school being simply the thing that happens for several hours before practice.

"How did you take all those years spent chasing football, and all the stuff you learned in football, and apply it to your writing career?" asks one Lane player. It is a stunningly insightful question, and one I'd never thought about other than in broad, conceptual ways. The fact of the matter is, to be good at either thing requires maniacal, laser-like focus, the ability to endlessly collaborate, and a punching-bag-like ability to take beatings and keep coming back for more. Writing and football are tailor-made for masochists.

"You know how, during two-a-days, when you're so tired every part of your body hurts—and even your teeth hurt?" I ask. "When you've had a tough practice, when the coach grabs your facemask and screams at you in front of your teammates, and you're embarrassed, and you call your mom at night and tell her to come get you?" They are nodding and laughing. I'm thinking back to every dehumanizing morning, when a coach would walk through the dorm with an air horn to wake us up; every sprint run for a stopwatch; and every long, sad, and lonely drive home from every "open tryout" that didn't pan out. "That's the part that helps, believe it or not. I've *almost* quit writing more times than I can remember—after a hurtful review, or after a rough e-mail from an editor. But the ability to keep going—to keep putting one foot in front of the other—that's what football teaches."

It's odd to be talking about football at a time in life when I'm so actively trying to extricate myself from it, and at a time when society is as obsessed with it as they've ever been. ESPN and the NFL Network are now in the business of airing college "pro days," where scouts and draft-eligible players gather for an event that is somewhere between meat market and theater of the absurd. These events have been called the "Underwear Olympics" for the way that the athletes strip to a pair of spandex shorts in order to run, jump, and lift in front of a bunch of older men—all of whom are still wearing all of their clothes. This coming on the heels of the NFL Scouting Combine in Indianapolis, which is another version of the exact same thing.

The Ole Miss pro day is especially strange that way. Ole Miss was the last SEC football program to integrate (in 1972), and its erstwhile mascot, Colonel Reb, stood as a sort of awkward reminder of the state's complicated history of racism and oppression. Colonel Reb was replaced, in 2010, by the kind of bland, achingly politically correct mascot—Rebel, the Black Bear—that somehow highlights and even makes worse the awkwardness of the previous mascot simply by sucking so badly. There was an Ole Miss student contingent that lobbied heavily for *Star Wars* character Admiral Ackbar to become the new face of Ole Miss football.

Today, the diasporic tribe of NFL scouts has descended upon Oxford, Mississippi, to watch young black men strip to their spandex underwear and run inside a multi-million-dollar, gleaming athletic facility. It's all just so weird—this sport that on one level is a trophy of racial reconciliation but on another is a reminder of everything we (as a culture) need to change. The news of the day is wide receiver Laquon Treadwell's disappointing 4.63-second forty-yard dash.

People watch because fans, and scouts, have an insatiable appetite for information. Young players watch because they one day dream of being on that kind of a stage, with that kind of opportunity.

I see these sorts of dreams in the eyes of Lane College's journalism students. They want what we all want, and what I desperately wanted at their age: to exist, to be known, and to be a little bit less anonymous. As silly as it sounds, I thought football—and snapping—would do that for me. It is a hope that is shared by every guy I've written about on these pages. It is both honorable and crazy. It is the kind of thing I want my sons to dream with all their hearts and then eventually grow out of. But it is, as all wish-dreams are, a very hard thing to grow out of.

After my talk I walk out of the building with a former Lane offensive lineman named Shaquille in a Chicago Bulls jacket. He is large—as in fill-the-doorframe large. He takes a business card and says he wants to get in touch about his writing. He stopped playing football after his freshman season, explaining that he wanted to "stop running my head into things." This makes me smile. Again, I can relate. I walk a few strides ahead of him, to catch the door, though I can sense him eyeing me.

"I knew you were a football player, man," he says.

"How?"

"Because of the way you walk."

This, again, makes me smile.

NOTES

INTRODUCTION

1. Being invited to speak at Blackford's graduation ceremony has long been my own personal, internal barometer of success. That is, were I ever invited to speak at the event, it would be a confirmation that in the eyes and hearts of my fellow hometowners, I was successful. In reality, my fellow hometowners probably don't care a whole lot one way or the other, because the graduation speaker is generally just the guy standing between them and lots of beer later in the evening.

I. WALKING ON BROKEN GLASS

1. George Plimpton was the editor of *The Paris Review* and had a serious literary rep, in addition to being a guy who occasionally wrote amazing, long-form, immersive stuff for *Sports Illustrated*. Plimpton's "thing" became participatory journalism in which he would embed, for a time, with a professional team or seek out opportunities to compete against pro athletes. The most famous example of this is a book called *Paper Lion* in which Plimpton participated in the Detroit Lions training camp in 1963 and wrote a book about the experience. My dad bought me a copy of the book once, after a business trip, and I have read it nearly every fall since, given that it has not only serious literary good vibes but also (now) a serious nostalgia factor. I love it.

4. THE CAUTIONARY TALE

1. In the oddest of postfootball twists, Strahan was a cohost with Kelly Ripa on the kind of banal, constant, without-end morning talk show on such topics as Kelly's childhood crush (Jason Bateman) and what to wear to the beach. In this, Strahan sort of went from doing one of the most dangerous things in the world for a living to doing the safest and most boring thing.

5. THE RUBIO ZONE

1. Pardee's grandfather, Jack Pardee, was an All-American linebacker at Texas A&M before embarking on a long and decorated NFL career in which he would distinguish himself as a player for the Washington Redskins, along with head coaching stops at the University of Houston, the Chicago Bears, and the Houston Oilers.

2. Though, to be clear and fair, his product is very, very good.

8. NOLAN OWEN

1. As it turns out, by press time, Owen has joined forces with Rubio—essentially heading the Rubio "franchise" in the Chicago suburbs. His new URL is http://www.rubiocoachnolanowen.com/.

10. THE PRIVATE LESSON

1. Beach training, as far as I can tell, involves running around and throwing passes but doing so in the water, at a beach.

11. THE RUBIO CAMP

1. Pepper has since signed with Kelli Masters Management, a sports representation firm with a small roster of current NFL clients and 2016 NFL draft prospects.

15. WHERE'D EVERYONE GO?

1. Rodger Sherman, "The NFL's Secret Disaster Scenario Is an Injured Long Snapper," SB Nation, December 15, 2015, http://www.sbnation.com/.

16. MOBILE AND THE NATURE OF EMBARRASSMENT

1. Though, to be clear, he's not the guy wearing the Jets swag all the time.

ABOUT THE AUTHOR

Ted Kluck's work has appeared in *ESPN the Magazine*, *Sports Spectrum Magazine*, and on ESPN.com. He currently serves as assistant professor of journalism at Union University and received an MFA in creative nonfiction from Ashland University.

His first book, *Facing Tyson: 15 Fighters, 15 Stories*, was published in October 2006, and internationally in 2007. His next two books, *Paper Tiger: One Athlete's Journey to the Underbelly of Pro Football* and *Game Time: Inside College Football*, were released in September 2007. *Why We're Not Emergent (by Two Guys Who Should Be)* was released in 2008 and won a Christianity Today award for book of the year in the church/pastoral leadership category. The follow-up title, *Why We Love the Church*, won the same award in 2009.

Ted's collection of sports essays, titled *The Reason for Sports*, was released in 2009, and his book on international adoption, called *Hello I Love You*, dropped in 2010. Ted has ghostwritten for a variety of clients, including Hall of Fame quarterback Jim Kelly and award-winning filmmaker Brian Ivie. He has written biographies of Robert Griffin III and Jeremy Lin.

In 2010 Ted founded Gut Check Press, an independent publishing house, where he holds the titles of cofounder and secretary of the interior. The company has released several titles including *The Christian Gentleman's Smoking Companion* and a rapture satire titled *Re: Raptured*. He is cohost of two successful podcasts: *The Happy Rant* and *The Gut Check Podcast*. Read more at http://www.gutcheckpress.com/.

Ted has played professional indoor football, coached high school football, trained as a professional wrestler, served as a missionary, and taught writing courses at the college level. He lives in Jackson, Tennessee, with his wife Kristin and sons Tristan and Maxim. He's a frequent speaker at conferences and events. Book Ted at http://www.tedkluck.com/.

2-17

NK